Imagination

Imagination

BEST STORIES BY

VILLAGE WRITERS

To order additional copies of this book, contact:
Xlibris Corporation
1-888-795-4274
www.Xlibris.com
Orders@Xlibris.com
25266

Contents

Dedication

Sincere Thanks To

D. Forrester Newhall, an experienced and prolific writer. She edited and re-typed every manuscript.

Jon David Douglas, a published novelist, worked endlessly with yet more typing, then transferring the entire book to a master disc.

Joann Sloan helped generously typing re-writes, never complaining about the time she spent doing so much to help the book's progress.

And finally, thanks to Glen West, boss of the Creative Writers, who trusted that we all would do our best.

Joan Heavey
Editor of Imagination!

WELCOME TO THE CREATIVE WRITERS GROUP STORYBOOK

Alan Gold of New York established the group some years ago and ably led it through its formative years. After his passing, I was appointed to continue his work. It has been my pleasure to encourage growth and attract new writers from all genres to our core group. In this volume our present eclectic membership is reflected in the selection of memoirs, stories and poems we have chosen for your reading enjoyment. The published works of several of our writers are available at The Bookworm on Main Street in The Villages, Florida.

Glen West, Moderator
Creative Writers Group

Biography of
Donald Phelps

Don Phelps's story is the first chapter of his novel-in-progress *The Reluctant Rebel*. The book narrates a young man's adventures and dangerous encounters during the first years of the American Revolution, in particular the growing conflict between families on the frontier and the battles they were forced to fight. He describes the battles of Saratoga and Oriskany, the latter claimed by many historians to be the bloodiest conflict of the Revolution.

Don has lived and worked as a journalist in this land that was America's frontier in Revolutionary times. He's walked its trails and battlefields and has learned 'secrets' that history books don't tell. From his novels, we the readers, learn all about these tantalizing secrets – and more, because Don tells his stories through fictional characters.

Phelps arrived at The Villages from New Jersey after having spent most of his career as a public relation's man in New York City, writing for major companies and 3 organizations.

RELUCTANT REBEL

Fiction

by Don E. Phelps

Daniel Sullivan probed the imprint of the fresh track in the soft ground, feeling the resilience of the damp, dark earth against his fingers.

She wasn't far ahead. He'd catch her soon. When he did . . . she'd pay!

Cutting a switch from a nearby bush, he followed her tracks up the hill. At its crest he paused, bringing the long switch to his shoulder, like a musket, sighting down its length at an imaginary deer.

Slowly, reluctantly . . . he lowered it. It wasn't fun pretending anymore, not like it used to be. Reality kept getting in the way and he couldn't ignore it.

Reality, he knew, lay in the valley below him. He looked down into it and saw what he always saw: the boredom of unbroken forests, the meandering flow of the Mohawk River by the old fort, smoke from cabins down in German Flats.

Daniel trudged on, following her tracks down the hill into the valley, his bony frame revealing some of the man he'd soon become.

"A strange one!" That's what people said.

Some claimed it was because his father raised him alone in the settlement farthest west of Albany. No! Their cabin was beyond the settlement. His father, Phares, wouldn't live in a settlement. He, too, was strange. One couldn't blame his boy for being that way.

Folks didn't know much about his mother. They had learned not to ask.

Daniel wasn't dumb. He was, in fact, far smarter than most folks. He could read and write, even cipher with ease. Blame his book-reading father for that too. For, whatever the reason, Daniel Sullivan seemed to develop slower than most. The fact he was still called "boy" testified to that. At his age, males in the Mohawk Valley were men.

The bursting promise of spring was all around Daniel, but he didn't see it. He didn't see the unfurling leaves that created soft green clouds on the horizon, nor did he notice that the once-naked branches of the hedgerow at the edge of the meadow were now covered with a thick, concealing growth.

Daniel saw no need to look. It was like a thousand other springs. This spring of 1775 was no different . . . nothing special.

Her tracks took him into a meadow, and he followed, walking close to the bushes that marked its edge, thinking what he would do with the switch when he caught her.

He saw movement in the bushes ahead and hurried forward, his eyes fixed on the swaying branches, ignoring everything else. He had almost reached them when the arm closed around his neck from behind, cutting off breath and sound in a single motion.

Daniel sucked for air: it brought the smell of sweat and campfires.

Instinctively he struck back with his elbows. Hitting nothing, he kicked back with his feet, searching for the legs behind him. In vain, he struggled against a powerful grip that would not give.

His face slammed into the earth as he was thrown to the ground. A knee pressed hard between his shoulders, and his head was pulled back roughly by the hair. Out of the corner of his eye he saw the quick flash of a knife, and terror griped him with the thought of what was happening: he was being scalped alive.

His injured throat wouldn't let him cry out, and because he couldn't scream the thought was more frightening.

He felt a sharp ripping at the top of his skull . . . then his head snapped forward and the knee was gone from his back.

For long moments, Daniel lay unmoving in the soft grass of the quiet meadow. Then, with hesitant fingers, he reached slowly for his sore head. To his surprise he felt no blood. Instead of wetness there was hair: short and bristly – but hair.

Laughter exploded behind him, and he rolled onto his back, looking up at the big man who stood over him, muscles outlined by the shrunken buckskin that molded his body. In one hand the man held a thick clump of Daniel's long black hair.

"Not a bad scalp," chuckled the man, "but I'm getting careless. Didn't cut close enough." He seemed to be studying the hair, but when Daniel kicked out at him, he sidestepped with the quickness of a young man, although his gray-streaked hair and grizzled beard said otherwise.

"Why'd you do it?" croaked Daniel, coughing out the words and swallowing hard before he could speak again.

"How many times do I have to tell you?" said the man, thrusting the black thatch toward Daniel. "Never let your guard down, no matter where you are. Never!" The tone of the man's voice and the look in his iron-gray eyes left Daniel no choice. He took the hair and, with a sound of disgust, threw it into the bushes.

"You had no right to do that to a man," he said.

"Didn't do it to a man," said the buckskinned figure, slipping his knife into its sheath and extending his hand to help Daniel up. "Did it to a boy . . . who wasn't paying attention."

"Damn!" said Daniel; hurt by the reference he was less than a man.

"There are two ways to learn: the easy way and the hard way. Your Pa and me taught you better. Keep your wits about you when you're in the woods."

"This ain't woods . . ."

"Don't make no nevermind," said the man, reaching into the bushes for his rifle. "Be ready everywhere. Be ready all the time . . ." The man smiled, and the crinkles around his eyes gave his tanned face the look of the wrinkled buckskin he wore. "Now! Move your lanky hide and go get that cow you've been chasin'. I want to see your Pa. It's been a while."

Phares Sullivan, oblivious of the buzzing flies, sat dozing on a three-legged stool, waiting for his son to bring in the cow. A wooden bucket sat within easy reach of his field-worn hands; his rounded shoulders rested against the logs of the little barn.

Some could remember how he came to the Mohawk Valley from Ireland, twenty years before, with nothing but a bundle of books over his shoulder and strange ideas in his head. To everyone's surprise, almost overnight, he became a frontiersman to rival them all.

A war whoop suddenly filled the tiny building, echoing off its rough – hewed walls, sending the horse plunging in its stall and chickens scattering in the barnyard. But Phares Sullivan didn't move a muscle.

"Noah Wayne!" he said, opening one unconcerned eye. "Still playing Indian?"

Noah Wayne set his flintlock by the door and shook Phares' hand, pleasure radiating from his worn face. "Beats knocking. Gets more attention."

"And someday it will get you killed," said Phares.

Behind Noah, Daniel eased into the barn, his hand trying to hide his missing hair.

"Your son thinks I'm all Injun. Says I tried to scalp him."

"Appears you did," said Phares. "Nobody's buying scalps these days. Why you taking them?"

Noah looked hurt. "After us teaching him to take care of hisself in the woods, I found him lollygagging along, thinking about everything but what he should be thinking. He needed a lesson."

"Weren't you a might hard on the boy, Noah?"

"Good God!" exclaimed Noah. "Look at him! Another year and he'll be bigger than both of us; that is, if somebody don't lift his hair for real."

Daniel put the cow in the stanchion and took the bucket and stool from his father. "Indians don't scalp anymore. Just old white men trying to relive the past," he said.

"There's still plenty who will," said Noah. "They just ain't doin' it now." He thrust a broad finger at Daniel. "It won't always be that way. Times are changin'" Noah gave Phares an imploring look. "Ain't this boy of yours got any sense?"

Phares put a hand on his friend's shoulder. "Daniel knows things. He can milk, scythe, stack, plant, hoe and spell better than you. That's what counts today, not Indian fighting. There hasn't been Indian trouble in years."

"Damn it, Phares! You and your fool notions, making the boy a farmer instead of lettin' him live off the land like a man's suppose to."

"If farming isn't living off the land, I don't know what is. I'm a farmer now and I reckon that's what Daniel will be if he's lucky. What's more, I'm a farmer with a thirst. Come up to the cabin. There's a jug I've been saving for your homecoming."

He gently pushed Noah through the doorway and turned to study Daniel's hair, bristles standing like wheat stubble. "Mind what Noah said, Daniel. You've had a hard lesson." He sensed his son had heard enough. "When you're finished, put the milk in the springhouse. Bring along a pitcher of the cold for supper."

After his father left, the cow bumped Daniel, reaching for hay in the manger. Daniel hit her as hard as he could. "Get over there, you son of a bitch! Get over and stop bothering me!"

The blaze in the fireplace lit the cabin, darting into dark corners and then retreating to let the blackness regain its rightful place. Pulse like, the dancing light expanded and contracted.

Phares, Noah and Daniel sat at the rough-plank table: Noah leaned back with his feet up. Phares cushioned his head in his hands, Daniel slouched between them, ignoring them both. Their backs were to the cabin's gloom: their feet reached toward the fire. They sat in silence, soaking up head against the chill of the spring night, letting the flickering fingers of light caress them.

Noah broke the mood by reaching for the stone jug beside him. "Could have used a little of this last winter . . ." He put a finger into the small loop on the jug's neck and tipped it up with his elbow, letting the contents gurgle into a drinking cup made from cow's horn, one end plugged with a circle of hand – carved hardwood to keep the liquid from leaking out. He drank deeply.

"Why'd you go off?" asked Phares. "You could have spent the winter by the fire, like me."

"Ain't no trappin' round here anymore, least none that amounts to much. Got to go where the fur is to make money." Noah reached into the deerskin shoulder bag lying on the floor at his feet. "Without money I can't buy presents."

He tossed a clumsily wrapped package on the table. It clunked heavily in front of Daniel who pulled at one edge of the paper. It unrolled and a long-bladed knife fell out. He picked it up, the bone handle smooth in his hand, ten inches of bright metal sparkling in the firelight.

"Thanks," he said, not taking his eyes from the treasured gift.

Noah laughed. "Since you're as big as a man, you should have a man's knife. It's just the thing for cuttin' hair."

Daniel looked up and smiled.

"What did you bring me?" teased Phares, knowing that friendship was the only gift that ever passed between them.

Noah's answer didn't hold the humor Phares expected. "I bring word trouble's comin'," said Noah in a voice that added to the chill of the room. "Took my furs to Albany this year because the price warn't much good at Johnstown."

"All the way to Albany? You haven't been there in years. You said it was too civilized."

"Still is! More than ever. Growin' all the time. Full o noise, people . . . and news that war's comin'."

"Damn! Said Phares, bringing his cup down on the table with an unexpected force that split the thin cow horn around the wooden plug. Whiskey began to seep through the crack. "I've been afraid of that . . ."

Phares wiped at the spilled whisky with his sleeve, drained the broken cup and tossed it into the fire. Flames drank in the whiskey fumes, jumped drunkenly into the air and fell back to the ashes, while the thin cow horn curled and blackened.

Noah cleared his throat. "In Albany they say the new Philadelphia Congress is sendin' an army to Boston."

"Damned Congress," said Phares. "It was suppose to solve problems, not make them worse."

"They say Congress wants independence from England."

"Not likely! It only wants the English troops out of Boston, repeal of the Intolerable Acts and representation in Parliament. If it gets that, it will sing 'God Save the King.'"

"Congress says . . . people want liberty."

"Why? Most have more than they need. You go where you want, do what you want. Do you need more?"

"They say . . . soon . . . everybody's gonna have to choose."

"Choose what?"

"Wig or Tory! Since last month at Lexington and Concord people are fightin' about it in every tavern between here and Albany."

"Damn fools!" said Phares. "What do they know about Whigs and Tories?" He turned to Daniel. "Tell Noah what a Whig is, Daniel."

"Something you put on your head?"

Phares turned away as a grin slowly spread across Daniel's face. "Daniel only pretends not to know . . . most people really don't. Whigs and Tories are nothing but English politicians trying to get control of the government. When one's for something, the other's against it. Neither gives a damn about the colonies. Both are using us to get what they want."

Noah cut in. "They say Whigs are for more rights and against taxes."

"Sure they are! Because Tories are in power and they're not. If it were the other way around, the Wigs would be taxing and Tories would be your friend."

Noah waited until Phares was through. Then he asked the question he had come to ask. "Which side you choosin', Phares?"

There was a long silence before Phares answered, "Neither!"

"You'll have to choose, if it comes to fightin'."

"No I won't. I'll wait till everything blows over."

"An if it don't?"

"Then I'll be neutral."

Phares eyes met those of his old friend. "I can't fight against the only government I've ever known, the government of my father's fathers, and I won't fight against friends and neighbors who take the other side. It's a choice I won't make."

"There'll be a lot of pressure to do what other people think is right."

"There always is," said Phares.

The cabin darkened as the fire died. No one made an effort to put on another log. Noah reached for the jug. "Somethin' else troubles me," he said. "Troubles me in a bug way. The Iroquois? What will they do if there's war?"

When Phares didn't answer, Noah continued. "Both sides will want the Injuns. And the side that gets 'em will most likely be the side that wins. What do you think the Iroquois will do?"

"What they've always done: play one side against the other to get what they can from both. They've been doing it for one hundred fifty years. Why would they stop now? Instead of French against English, it will be Whigs against Tories."

Phares chuckled. "The Iroquois are smarter than most people think. They'll be neutral like me. It's not their war anymore than it's mine."

"When it's counted," said Noah, "the Johnsons have always been able to bring them to the side of the English: twice against the French and even in Pontiac's uprising."

"If William Johnson were alive, he'd do it again. But he's been dead since last July. Neither Sir John nor Guy Johnson have the power over the Iroquois that Sir William had. The Iroquois would have followed him into hell. With him dead, they'll stay neutral until they know who's going to win . . ."

"And then?" asked Noah.

". . . then they'll join the winning side!"

"That's what I'd like to do."

"Then do it!" said Phares. "There's no reason you can't. This isn't New England. We've no trouble here."

Noah made the sound in his throat he always did when he openly disputed Phares. "I ain't bright," he said, "but I ain't dumb either. I survive in the woods by reading signs, and the signs say trouble's closer than you think."

Phares leaned back and braced himself for the news he knew Noah had been holding back. He smiled inwardly at how Indian-like Noah was with his patience and his ability to present the dramatic at the most appropriate moment. He almost expected Noah to reach into his war bag and throw down a belt of wampum for emphasis, as Indians sometimes did.

"Two days from now," said Noah, "the Whigs are raising a Liberty Pole at Caughnawaga: right in the middle of the Valley. It ain't but a hoot and a holler from Johnson Hall; it's practically in Sir John's backyard."

"Then I'm wrong." Said Phares. "Troubles here!"

Daniel's ears picked up for the first time during the long evening. He had heard his father and Noah argue many times about many things, but important things, not like tonight. Finally, though, Noah said something that interested him. Something new was about to happen. Something different. Something to relieve the dullness of his life.

"Can I go see them raise the Liberty Pole, Pa?"

"I'm goin'," said Noah.

Daniel looked at his father. "Can I, Pa?"

"We best stay out of this," said Phares. "It's not our business. We've trouble enough without looking for more."

Phares turned to Noah. "There will be trouble!"

"Most likely," said Noah.

"That Liberty Pole is the first challenge to King George's authority in the Mohawk Valley. The Johnsons can't let it happen. Guy Johnson will use those big tenant farmers Sir William brought from Scotland and it will be the biggest fight this Valley has ever seen."

Phares got up and went to the fireplace, his movements almost unseen in the darkened room. He dropped a log on the hot coals. The new blaze spotlighted him as he turned. "If people in the Valley raise a Liberty Pole, it will put us in the middle of a war we don't have to be in. Let New Englanders fight if they've a – mind; the Virginians too, if they want. I say it's not my fight, and I'm staying out of it."

Phares sat down at the table, fingers drumming on its rough boards. Noah said nothing.

"Can I go Pa? Can I go with Noah to the raising?" Daniel caught himself begging, almost like a child.

Phares looked up, annoyance plain on his face. "You haven't heard a word I said, have you?" He turned toward the fire and away from Daniel.

"You're getting big, Daniel. A man grown, almost. Like your scalping today, there are some things you're going to have to learn the hard way." He paused. "Go, if you're a-mind."

Phares got up and went to the cupboard to replace his broken cup. As he passed Noah, he said softly:

"Take care of him . . ."

Biography of
Claudia Cunningham

Claudia Cunningham is the senior member of the Creative Writer's Group. A bit past ninety, Claudia's poems and stories are a delight to those fortunate enough to hear, or read them. She was born and raised in Pittsburgh, Pennsylvania. Claudia's father was a newspaperman, her mother a professional photographer. She says she's been seriously writing for only the past twenty years, all the other stuff she wrote before that time got dumped in the trash. Now the writer's group waits anxiously to hear her next poem, or short story that are always polished and elegant, full of wisdom and wicked wit.

The Little Old Ladies

Poem

by Claudia Cunningham

Little old ladies,
Going out to lunch
Like twittering birds,
All in a bunch.

With purses too large
And hemlines that droop
Chattering happily
Off they troop.

The tall one in front
The plump one in back
The thin one in the middle
To take up the slack.

They're all helping Doris
To drive her own car:
"Watch out for that truck!"
"Have we driven too far?"

"Park near the door."
"No, under the tree!"
"Remember your coupons –
"You get dessert free!"

Little old ladies
Going out to lunch
Searching the menu
For goodies to munch.

Nothing too filling
Or hard to chew,
Not too expensive,
Will fruit salad do?

"Too much lettuce!"
"The dressing's too strong"
"And tomatoes with fruit
Is simply all wrong!"

"The cornbread is crumbly"
"Their iced tea is weak"
"The napkins too small,
Ineffectual and leak."

Bets wants dessert
Mary does not;
The pie is too much
For our tiny Dot.

"We two are together
And we had the lamb!"
"We are each separate"
I sent back my ham."

"You charged us for tea –
"We didn't have any!"
"You charged us over
"By a dime and a penny!"

The waitress is new
And thoroughly confused
While at the next table
The men are amused.

Bets sweeps the muffins
Into her purse
No change for a tip;
She whispers a curse.

The Little Old Ladies
Are now off to shop
In tennis shoes
And red ankle socks.

Searching each counter
All through the store
Hoping to remember
What they came in for.

Their rubber-tipped canes
Are going "Tap, tap, tap"
While their memory connectors
Are going "Snap, snap, snap!"

On the road home
The car's forward motion
Acts like a magic
Sleepy-time potion.

Jan's head sinks down
And she starts to doze
As her smart new hat
Slips down to her nose.

Betsy slumps over
And is starting to snore
While her purse full of muffins
Slips to the floor.

It's their once-a-week treat
Doing shopping and lunch
An exciting adventure
For this little bunch.

Sometimes they laugh
And sometimes they weep
When they're not nodding
Off to sleep.

Biography of
D. Forrester Newhall

D. Forrester Newhall was born and raised in San Francisco and is one of The Villages' most talented and prolific writers. After graduating from the Sarah Dix Hamlin School, she attended San Mateo College, majoring in English and History. D. Forrester lived in Europe for fourteen years and traveled extensively world wide. She's visited Greece, Egypt, (where she traveled by camel to see the Pyramids), India, Nepal, Thailand, Singapore and Hong Kong, plus most European countries. While living in England, she wrote a number of articles on Sighthounds, Coursing and Lure-coursing that were published in English dog magazines.

D. Forrester's new novel, just out, has the title *The Hunt is Away*. The book tells of exciting adventures and intelligence intrigues just after World War II, as a Communist faction tries to take over the Austrian government and kill a former intelligence agent Henri Bolkonsky, the main character of the story. The book can be purchased locally at local bookstores. A nearly-finished new novel *The Spider's Web* will be available next year.

BLAS

Fiction

by D. Forrester Newhall

The wind is blowing hard again tonight. I can almost hear the cold as it whistles around the eaves of the cottage. The wind also brings the howls of the great grey ghosts that live in the forest and mountains around me.

The great wolves are hungry and have come down from their fastness hoping to find food close to the village. This winter has been especially severe. It came early this year in a snowstorm that cut the village off from the rest of the world for a fortnight.

I have been sitting here by Nana's fire. She is asleep in a chair opposite me. The fire is hot and yet I feel cold. I know it is watching me. I can feel it's strange yellow eyes staring unblinkingly at my back. It watches me from the edge of the forest. I have seen it's prints in the snow on the edge of the clearing. I am afraid to turn my head for fear it will come closer.

I don't know why I am writing this. Lord knows nobody will ever read it and if, by chance, they do, they will never believe it. I must write it down or go mad. Maybe if I begin at the beginning it will all make sense.

As I stepped off the coach I saw him. He was leaning against a low stonewall, one hand in his stained leather trouser pocket, the other toying with a straw. He reminded me of an animal sunning itself on an early spring day. I immediately put him down as the village idler and turned my gaze over the square. It was typical of all mountain villages. The cobbles gleamed dully under the noon sun and looked as if they had been freshly washed. A large ornate stone fountain played musically in the center with a few brown-legged children laughingly splashing each other in its cool water. Whitewashed houses bordering the square had neat window boxes planted gaily with flowers. The steep gabled roofs mimicked the mountains surrounding them. A stone church, a hotel and a few small family-run shops completed the picture.

The trip from Budapest to this village in the high Tatras Mountains had been long and dreary. I was very tired but glad I had arrived safely. The roads were muddy and rutted with the early spring rains making the journey into the mountains rough and uncomfortable. As the coach pulled noisily away I looked around for Frau Neus who was to meet me, but all was quiet – only the children and the village idler were in sight. I was about to pick up my suitcase and walk to the hotel to wait when a deep voice stopped me. It sounded like the soft growl of a large dog.

"You are Janet?" The accent had been placed on the last syllable.

I turned startled, as I had seen no one enter the square. The village idler was standing just behind me. "Yes, I am Janet Jasko." I replied automatically.

He gave a slight nod of his head. "I am Blas." He leaned down to pick up my suitcase. I started to protest but he added as an afterthought, "Mother is waiting at the cottage."

"Oh! You are Nana's son." I exclaimed, smiling.

He turned his eyes full upon me in surprise at my ignorance, "Yes." And began to lope off across the cobbled square.

I followed him up a path between the houses. Halfway up the hill I regretted wearing my city heels instead of flats. Blas was now nearly to the top while I was already out of breath in this high altitude.

"Blas – Blas wait for a moment," I called.

He turned to look down at me. It was then that the first small inkling of fear touched me. I was looking against the sun and his thin body was like a black angular shadow against the meadows behind him. It seemed to me he was in a half crouched position reminding me of a large animal. I stood utterly still. I had an unaccountable urge to turn and run back to the safety of the hotel in the square. I shook myself, *'don't be an idiot. It is only Blas with my suitcase standing up there,'* I told myself and slowly started up the hill again laughing at my momentary imaginative fear.

Nana's cottage nestled in a meadow with the forest wrapping around it on three sides. Its whitewashed walls gleamed in the sun, dotted with window boxes planted with red, yellow and blue flowers. Almost like an artist had splashed brightly colored paint on a white canvas. The thatched roof hung low like a mop of unruly hair, giving it a homey air.

Nana was there to greet me and my uneasiness vanished. That night, as I sat in front of a log fire in Nana's house, I felt at peace for the first time in months. It was like old times with Nana fussing about and bringing me a cup of hot chocolate before bedtime. Nana, my nurse when I was a child, left to get married and have a family of her own when I was five. Since then we had corresponded regularly, and after my mother died, Nana suggested I come to her village for a rest and to get away from the old house and its memories of sickness. She did not have room in her small cottage for me but rented one close to hers.

Blas came in and crouched in front of the fire. Again I had the distinct feeling of looking at a large wild animal. The light on his face outlined his high cheekbones, the hollows of his cheeks, the long lean jaw line. His eyes did not blink at the fire. Then it struck me. They were yellow. Nana's large bustling figure coming through the door from the kitchen broke the momentary fear that again began to rise in me.

"How are the sheep, Blas?" the practical voice asked softly.

"Safe for now." Blas reached for the steaming mug of chocolate she handed him. "They are in the meadow."

"Who is with them tonight?"

"Jan and Christian." Blas turned his strange eyes towards the fire and cupped his hands around the mug.

"Good. The wolves are coming down early this year. We will have to put them in the fold sooner than usual."

"Wolves!" I exclaimed startled. "I didn't know there were any around here."

Blas turned his head with a strange smile on his lips. "Yes, they live up in the high mountains and rarely come down this far but there have been late heavy snows up there."

"It is going to be a hot summer and a hard winter this year." Nana added, then turned to look at me. "You have had a long hard journey Janny. I will take you over to the cottage. It should be warm by now."

"That's all right Nana I can find my way."

"No! It is not safe. Tomorrow we will go into the village and I will show you where to shop. In the meantime it is a warm bed and a good night's rest for you."

Meekly I followed her after saying goodnight to Blas. He did not seem to hear me but stared, as if mesmerized, into the fire. Nana bustled me further up the hill and into my cottage talking all the while. Gratefully I sank into the first really good deep sleep that I had had in almost a year. It was good to have someone else make the decisions, even to running me. I was so tired. So very, very tired – mentally and physically exhausted to the point of a nervous breakdown after nursing mother through her illness and death.

I can hear the howls coming closer – or is it the wind? I cannot tell, they intermingle so. The snow is coming down harder making a white, impenetrable wall beyond the window. I want to draw the curtains but I am afraid. Dear God what shall I do? My mind keeps jumping from one thing to another. I cannot concentrate.

For the first few weeks, after I arrived, I stayed close to the cottages and Nana. We went shopping in the village and I started to relax. Slowly the sun warmed my body and the valley and mountains brought peace to my soul. Life flowed at an even steady pace.

There was only one thing that disturbed the tranquility of my mind – Blas. He rarely spoke and then only in short sentences. He was a strange lonely person. His days were spent out in the fields and at night he sat – no that is not the word – crouched by the fire. Not once did he go down to the village of an evening to drink beer with the other men. They seemed to stand in awe of him. I noticed that if he happened to pass a group of villagers they always fell silent until he was well beyond. Then, and only then did they continue their conversation again. Blas seemed not to notice and paid them no heed. Several times I saw one or two of the women surreptitiously cross themselves when his back was turned.

One day, when I was helping Nana hang out the wash, she said, "Janny would you take Blas his dinner? He forgot it this morning and I can not leave the baking."

I hesitated before answering, "All right."

Apparently Nana heard it in my voice for she added, "Besides the walk will do you good. You need to exercise and get the blood moving in your body."

"Where is he?"

"In the high meadow. He will be bringing some of the young lambs down later this afternoon." Quickly Nana filled a small tin jug full of tea and took a small parcel wrapped in a printed scarf from the table.

"How do I find my way there?" I asked taking them from her.

"See that path into the woods?" Nana said pointing. "Take that and follow it to the other side. There will be a meadow beyond and another patch of woods. You will not miss the path through them. Blas will be in the meadow on the other side."

Nana was already hanging out the rest of the wash by the time I reached the first path. Cool shadings of green and brown enveloped me as I stepped out of the brilliant sunlight. Great pines rose above me their branches intertwined overhead. Shafts of sunlight struck through the trees like shaded light through a high window. My footsteps were deadened by the thickly needle-carpeted ground. Only the call of a bird or a snap of a twig broke the silence which surrounded me. I delighted in this cool silence and the smell of wet pine and rich earth.

The path which I followed wound back and forth following the contours of the land. It was hard for me to realize that I was climbing, so gently did it rise. I walked slowly, savoring this peaceful time. Nothing, I thought could be as beautiful as this. A joy, such as I had not known for a long time, rose within me. I wanted to run, to throw my arms around these trees and valleys and mountains. My whole being seemed suffused and I smiled and laughed out loud in pure happiness.

As I turned a bend in the path I caught my breath in awe. Ahead a meadow appeared with a riot of wild flowers blanketing it. The mountains rose in white – topped jagged walls. The meadow was shaped like a bowl, trapping the warmth of the sun. Bees darted from flower to flower humming their busy little tunes. As I stepped into this idyllic setting I could just see the woods on the other side. They provided a dark green, almost black, curtain to the gold and lavender field. I stood in wonder gazing at this perfect spot, and was reluctant to move on. I wanted to stay in this beautiful place but knew I had to leave it. I began to slowly cross the meadow, not really wishing to enter the forest beyond.

I must have been about halfway across when I sensed a movement on the edge of the forest. I stopped, shading my eyes to see what it was, but the movement ceased. *'It's just a bird flitting through the trees,'* I thought, yet I hesitated to go on. Giving myself a good shake I resolutely started forward, but the nearer I came to the forest the more dark and forbidding it seemed. My steps began to slow until I came to a halt altogether. I was no more than a few yards from its edge and could just see a barely discernable dark path. I had an eerie feeling I was looking down a dark tunnel or a cavern with no end.

'This is ridiculous!' I said aloud to myself. *'Your imagination is working overtime. Now stop it!',* but I could not still the dread which I now felt. I looked right and left, but saw no way to skirt the forest. I must go through it to reach the meadow and Blas. At the thought of him my apprehension rose another notch.

'Stop this at once, Janny' I said to myself and resolutely started forward once more. *'You are driving yourself into a panic. It is silly and stupid. These woods are just like the other ones. No different, and that one didn't scare you so why should this?'* I kept talking aloud to myself.

It did not help. This forest was different. No shafts of sunlight penetrated through the trees to light the path. The trees were bigger, older, and grew closer together, interlocking their branches overhead in a dark impenetrable roof. The bushes were thicker and no sound could be heard. I stopped to listen, but all was silence. Silence so complete, like total deafness. No bird winged its way through these trees. No animal moved through the brush. The silence bore down on me like a thick suffocating blanket.

It took some time for my eyes to adjust to the gloom after the bright sunlight of the meadow. I stopped and looked back, but the path had twisted so I could not see it. I hurried on, still talking to myself in a low monotone. The barely discernable path twisted around the base of the trees and I lost my bearings completely. Roots seemed like traps as I stumbled over them and low branches caught at my dress and hair. I cried out as I fell, twisting my ankle. Pain stabbed along my leg and I sat up and rubbed it. "Damn! Now I suppose I have broken it." I said aloud. Tears sprang to my eyes as I tried to stand. "What am I going to do if I can't walk on it? I certainly can't stay here. This is about the most deserted spot I have ever seen." I eased my leg and foot into a more comfortable position and leaned against a tree. "This is a fine fix. The meadow can't be too far away, but there is no use calling. Who would hear? Perhaps Blas. Nana said he was bringing some young lambs down to the fold, but he may take another way down." I frowned as I took my kerchief and wound it around my foot and ankle. "There has to be another path. I can't see herding sheep along this one. Why didn't I think of that back in the meadow? I should have looked for it. Stupid!"

I started and turned my head. A twig snapped and in this stillness it sounded like a shot. I started to call out but my cry strangled in my throat. Overwhelming fear clutched at me. I heard the soft pad of a step upon the path. Slowly, very softly I pushed myself to a standing position, my back scraping along the rough bark of the tree. I stared down the path, but could see nothing. The padding tread stopped. No sound came to my ears. It was as if whoever or whatever it was, was also listening.

Very carefully I moved away from the tree, still staring down the path behind me. There was deathly silence. I came to almost believe I had imagined the noise when I heard the soft brush of a body against some bushes. This time the noise was much nearer. Was it a deer or some other animal? Fear rushed through me and I whirled, stumbling blindly down the path, not stopping to look back. The pain in my ankle was lost in my panicked dash. The thudding of my heart and my labored breathing, as I gulped in air, smothered any noise of a pursuer.

I became dimly aware that the trees were thinning and the dark world through which I had come was beginning to lighten. My eyes seemed to focus for the first time since my blind panic back on the path. It was definitely lighter. Sunlight filtered through the trees and I could distinguish shapes. As I turned a bend in the path I thudded into something. It was hard and yet yielding. There was an animal smell of warm wool, sweat and earth. Strong bands of steel closed about me imprisoning my arms. Strange yellow eyes looked down at me. I screamed and tried to pull away but I could not move. Then a black haze closed over my eyes and I fainted.

There is something I must remember. Something about that day. It is important but I can't remember. It has to do with voices talking. Blas seemed to be talking to someone but the voices were only his low growling voice. Yet it was a conversation. Someone else was there I'm sure. Two people talking with one voice. I vaguely remember being carried and the smell of wool, earth and sweat. Clear memory only returned when I woke up in Nana's bed back at the cottage.

I had only lightly sprained my ankle and was soon moving with comparative ease. I began to take walks across the meadows stopping to pick wild flowers or just standing and gazing at the mountains. In the evenings I sat by Nana's fire sewing or holding her yarn while she rolled it into a ball. Sometimes I would read aloud to her or, like Blas, simply watch the flames making pictures as they leaped and changed.

As the summer wore on my latent fear of Blas was always present, but at the same time I was curious about him. I even took to carrying his lunch to him. When I first suggested it to Nana she gave me a startled look then smiled to herself. When I asked her why she smiled, shrugged her shoulders and said, "No reason, Janny." And left it at that.

Blas didn't say anything when I first went to the high meadow. He just grunted, opened the kerchief and began to eat, his eyes constantly roving over the sheep as if continually counting them. I lingered a while asking questions about them but he only answered "Yes" or "No" in that deep monosyllabic growl. Most times he didn't answer at all.

One day as I was walking up to the meadow, I picked some flowers near the woods intending to take them back to Nana. Blas barely turned his head when I came up. I sat on the grass beside him chatting about nothing hoping to draw him out. As he finished his lunch he said, "Those flowers will wilt to nothing before you get back," and slowly walked over to a little stream.

I hadn't thought he had noticed them, and was unaccountably pleased that he had. He came back with the kerchief-dripping wet. As he reached out to take them from my hand he stopped suddenly. His whole body seemed to become rigid, his strange eyes narrowing. Then with a sudden movement he snatched them from my hand and threw them as far as he could. Turning on me he snarled, "Get back to the cottage and don't come up here again."

"Why? Blas, why?" I backed away from him in terror.

"Little fool! You picked wolfs bane. Do as I say." He growled, gave me another look, then turned and loped off up the hill. And so for a time, I let it be.

Three days ago I took Blas his lunch for the first time in weeks. Nana was in the village buying winter supplies. It was bitter cold and I wrapped my coat tightly about me, a shawl over my head.

Blas seemed angry when he saw me and didn't give me a chance to explain. "Go back to the cottage quickly," he snarled as he grabbed his lunch out of my hands. "I told you not to come up here again." As he turned to go he said over his shoulder, "Tell mother I am bringing the last of the sheep down the mountain and will be in late."

I went angrily back the way I came, furious with Blas for his surliness. *'I was only doing him and Nana a favor by bringing him his lunch,'* I thought as I stomped along. *'He didn't have to be so rude! At least he could have said thank you.'*

The wind blew in gusts and snow clouds scudded across the sky. I pulled my shawl more closely about me, for the weak winter sun gave no warmth. The air seemed to grow colder the closer I got to the woods where I sprained my ankle.

It was across the meadow just by the woods that I saw it. I cannot describe what it was – animal or human. It did not move but seemed to stare in my direction. I knew instinctively that the creature was the personification of evil but I could not move. I wanted to run to the cottage but it was beyond the woods and the creature was between it and me. I was too afraid to turn back to Blas so I stood rooted where I was.

Even as I watched the creature seemed to disappear, melting into the underbrush behind it. I stayed where I was for a long time staring at the spot. I felt icy cold. Finally I started to edge along the woods surrounding the meadow until I came to the wide grassy path Blas had shown me. I walked quickly, then ran.

Fear snapped at my heels as I ran, my breath coming in heaving gasps. As I turned a corner in the path I saw a man kneeling over something. I stopped only a few yards away. Something about the clothes and back seemed familiar.

"Blas?" I called tentatively, "how did you get here before me?"

The man sprang up, whirling towards me. The face was like Blas', but there was something different about it. The eyes were the same – that same strange yellow color with slit-like pupils. The mouth was drawn back showing deeply stained teeth. It was then that I knew real terror.

We stood staring at each other for a minute before he moved slowly towards me. I could hear the low rasp of his breathing and it was then that I noticed the blood on his arms and chest. I screamed and whirled but his hand clamped over my shoulder jerking me back against him. I remember screaming again before I fainted.

There was a smell of animals, wool, earth and sweat as I slowly swam back to daylight. Distantly I made out the sound of a deep growling voice. I was lying in a meadow. I started to struggle to sit up but strong hands held me down and a voice kept repeating, "Quiet, Janny, you are safe now."

I opened my eyes. Blas was leaning over me, a wet kerchief in his hand. Gently he placed it against my temples. For a moment I saw his face soften and his eyes become gentle, then the look was gone as fleeting as a breeze. When I looked again his face returned to its normal mysterious remoteness, as hard and unreadable as rocks.

"Blas. What happened?" I asked as I struggled to a sitting position. "What were you doing on the path?"

"I was not on the path." He growled turning away.

"But I saw you!"

"I found you unconscious here in the meadow."

"But you were on the path." I insisted, "I saw you. You were bending over something and when you turned there was blood on your chest and arms." I protested. "I became frightened and started to run away but you grabbed me and I fainted."

"You imagine things." Blas turned back towering over me. "Now come. I will take you back to the cottage."

"But . . ." The look on his face stopped me as he pulled me to my feet. We walked back in silence, or rather Blas loped ahead while I followed.

Nana fussed about me as usual and would not listen to my explanation. But I saw a look pass between her and Blas when they thought I was not watching. Later that night when Blas came back he spoke quietly to Nana. I caught the word 'wolfs bane' and 'Vlad', but that was all.

"Wolfs bane". That word keeps returning. Why? I looked it up. It is a purplish blue flower, hood shaped, that grows in the mountains. But why would Blas react so violently? And what was he doing on the path? I know it was Blas. I cannot have been mistaken. Is Blas two persons? The one I know – Nana's son? The Shepherd? And the one I saw on the path? The one who terrifies me? How can he move so fast, as if he were in two places at once?

The village was in an uproar yesterday. One of the shepherds was killed. They found his body in a patch of woods. They say it was the wolves, or rather one lone wolf. I saw the women crossing themselves as they clustered in groups whispering about it. It was strange. Whenever I came near they would look at me and move away. Their whispers started up again after I passed, just as they do when Blas is near. Even the men seem afraid.

This evening I was at Nana's as usual. She is not well so I did not stay long after supper. Nana did not want me to walk back to my cottage by myself. Queer. She has been hovering over me ever since that day I took lunch up to Blas. Hovering not in a maternal way but protectively, as if in fear something will happen. Nana knows something and so does Blas and they are keeping it from me. What is it?

"Janny, wait until Blas comes back. He will walk you to the cottage."

"Oh! Nana. I'm all right. Do stop worrying about me." I laughed. "It is not far."

Nana's worried face looked up at me from her chair by the fire. The firelight seemed to highlight the soft aging lines about her eyes and mouth. Perhaps it was that she was not well. She seemed to have aged more in these past few days. "Janny, please wait. It is not safe for you to be out alone."

"Nana, the villagers say the wolf has gone so there is nothing to worry about. It is only a few hundred yards and I cannot possibly get lost. I am tired and you must rest." Resolutely I moved towards the door. "Goodnight, Nana."

"Janny." Nana called just as I reached for the latch. She held out a small silver cross on a silver chain. "Take this. Put it around your neck."

"But Nana, that is yours. You have always worn it!"

"I shall not need it much longer. I want you to have it and wear it always. Never take it off. It is my gift to you."

Smiling I clasped it around my neck. "Thank you, Nana. I promise to always wear it." As I bent down and kissed her I thought I caught the gleam of a tear in her eye, but when I looked again she was smiling gently.

"Oh! Nana. It is a beautiful night." I exclaimed as I opened the door. "The moon is full and makes the snow so white. Like sparkling sugar. What a perfect night." I turned and blew her a kiss, stepped onto the porch and shut the door.

For a few minutes I stood there gazing over the white landscape. The woods made a black backdrop to the snowy stage. The mountains rose in black and white layers reaching up into the starlit sky. The wind blew gently through the trees causing small showers of snow to fall from their branches. Everything was peaceful, quiet, crisp and clean. I wrapped my scarf more tightly around my neck and started up the path. The snow squeaked and crunched with each step I took.

My little cottage stood back off the path in a small clearing. I could see its comfortable plump outline from where I stood. A light was shining through one of the windows welcoming me home. But this time instead of dancing across the clearing, as I would have on a night such as this I stood still, pressing myself against the trunk of a tree.

Against the light I saw the shape of an animal crouching very still beneath my window. My blood ran cold. As I watched, the creature stealthily rose placing its paws upon the windowsill, and peered into the room. It swung its head back and forth as if looking for something.

For a moment, as it turned its head sideways, to my horror I realized it was not an animal at all, but a human. Blas' unmistakable profile was outlined against the light. He turned and started to move around the house but stopped, listening. In the silence I heard the distant call of the wolves. Blas raised his head towards the sky. I cannot say if the howl that screamed through the clearing came from Blas or from the wind which suddenly rushed through the trees. I turned and ran back to Nana's cottage praying the thing did not see me.

*   *   *

My hands were shaking as I locked and barred the door to Nana's cottage. The room was almost totally dark now. Nana had not lit the lamps and only the light from the fire illuminated a small area around the chairs. Nana was still where I had left her but from the door I could see only the outline of her body in the wing-backed chair.

"Janny, what's the matter?" Nana's disembodied voice sounded alarmed.

"He's out there!" I cried, "And he wants to kill me!" My whole body was shaking now and my knees felt as if they would buckle under me.

"Who is out there?"

"Blas."

"No, Janny. It is not Blas." Nana sighed and stirred.

"But I saw him! He was looking in the window of my cottage and then when he heard the wolves he howled back to them."

"Janny you are wrong."

"But I saw his face! I know it is Blas!"

"It is not Blas, Janny. Blas has been protecting you."

"What do you mean 'protecting' me? From what – from whom?"

"From Vlad, his twin brother." Nana pushed back the lap robe and rose with an effort. "Come sit by the fire and I will make some hot chocolate."

"Nana, I'm so confused. He seems to change shape – from wolf to man and back again. What is he? Am I imagining things?" Nana didn't answer but moved towards the kitchen. "I don't want any hot chocolate. I want to know what is going on. What is Vlad and why does he want to kill me?"

"Go sit by the fire and I will try to tell you."

When Nana came back she carried two steaming mugs. I curled up shivering in my chair, my heart still pounding. As she turned to sit opposite me I noticed, with a shock, she had aged drastically in the short time I had been gone. Her robust body had shrunk; her once dark hair was now almost all grey; her hands were smaller, coarser; and her eyes were paler. For a long time Nana stared into the fire, the look of her reminding me of Blas. When she finally spoke her voice too had changed.

Nana's Tale:

'Many centuries ago, during the Dark Ages, the land where we are now was wild. The forest was full of bears, wolves and boar. There were few villages and fewer people. It was a bloody time, full of superstition and fear, war, death and destruction. It was a time when people believed in witches and warlocks, vampires and werewolves, God and the Devil.' She sighed, 'Who knows if they weren't right?

'Stephan, my husband, whose family had lived in these mountains and forests for many generations, did not know when his ancestors came but believed it was during that period. From remembered time, and no doubt earlier, they have been woodcutters and shepherds, tending their own flocks as well as the village flocks.

'Somewhere back in the mists of time, tainted blood came into the family. How, no one knows, perhaps from the bite of some infected beast. The terrible result does not show up in every generation. It may skip a few then show up suddenly in another, so the birth of a child is not a time of rejoicing for us. It is a time of fear and uncertainty. When Blas and Vlad were born we did not know if the evil blood flowed in their veins; if both would be tainted or only one; or if by some miracle neither. It was when they were baptized that we found out. The Holy Water burned a deep scar in Vlad's forehead and a slight scar in Blas'. Both were tainted, Vlad terribly.

'Stephan wanted to take Vlad high up into the mountains and leave him. He would not – could not – kill him outright – but would leave the decision to God. I would not let him and kept both children close. Stephan felt Vlad was truly evil and rarely had anything to do with him.

'When they were two years old a band of Gypsies came through the valley. The Dom's wife gave me a talisman, a silver cross, one for each boy. They were to wear them all the time, never take them off. The talismans would win out over evil, she said.

'One day, when they were sixteen, Blas was in the village so Stephan took Vlad up to the high meadow to help with the sheep. Stephan never came home. Blas and I went to look for them and found Stephan dead, Vlad's cross lying nearby. I do not know what happened. I know Stephan hated Vlad and Vlad hated his father. I believe they had an argument; Vlad tore off the talisman and let his evil nature completely take over. I am sure he killed his father. After that Vlad disappeared and we did not see him for many years.

'One especially severe winter the wolves came down from the high mountains. They were led by a huge black wolf. They raided the village folds but never touched ours.

'That same winter Blas went into the forest to cut wood for the fire. There he encountered Vlad. Vlad boasted that he could change himself from man into wolf and back again at will. He told Blas he was the leader of the pack and tried to entice Blas into joining him. Blas refused.

'From time to time, over the years, Vlad would return. He would never come to the cottage but would confront Blas in the meadow or woods. Each time Vlad was more evil, more vicious.

'Last spring he saw you taking dinner to Blas and followed you. Blas warned him off; told him to leave you alone. Vlad wouldn't listen. Finally Blas told him you belonged to him, Blas. He hoped that would be the end of it, but it had the opposite effect. Vlad wants you to be his mate. That is why he is here now. So far Blas had stood between you and Vlad. How much longer I don't know.'

"What?" I stared at Nana horrified at the thought of this creature wanting me!

"He wants you because Blas wants you. He wants what he can't have, Janny. The cross I gave you will protect you from Vlad."

I was trying to take all this in, but the only thing I really understood was that Blas wanted me. It was then I realized that over the months, I had grown to love Blas. That is why I hadn't left for Budapest at the end of summer. Why I had stayed on. One thing still nagged at my mind. Why had Blas reacted so violently when I picked wolfs bane by mistake?

When I asked Nana she said, "It is a superstition that if you pick wolfs bane you will attract the wolfs attention and die violently. Blas was afraid for you, especially since Vlad was near by. Now it is all coming true, Janny. You must protect yourself."

The light from the fire grew dimmer as we talked. The howls of the wolves grew closer. "My cocoa is cold, Nana. Let me make some more for both of us and put more wood on the fire." Nana did not answer. I got up and went into the kitchen. As I boiled the milk I glanced out the window and saw movement at the edge of the clearing. One wolf appeared; then another and another until there were a dozen moving back and forth. They were silent now, but seemed to be moving with a purposefulness. The silence was more frightening than their howls.

I ran back to the room where Nana was and as I did a blast of cold air swept through. The door was wide open. As I rushed to close it I saw, not ten yards away, a small grey wolf trotting towards the woods. It was going away from the cottage and its prints led directly from the door where I stood. In confusion I called, "Nana, who opened the door?" The grey wolf stopped and looked back at me for a moment, then turned and went on. I softly closed the door and looked towards the fire. Nana's lap robe lay crumpled on the floor in front of her chair. I was completely alone.

I don't know how long I have sat here in the kitchen. The wolves have completely surrounded the cottage. I can't run to the village or to my cottage, but that wouldn't do any good anyway. They would just surround it and I would be trapped there the way I am here. Where is Blas? I wish he were here. I don't know what to do. I am so afraid; afraid to look out the window; afraid to move. I have locked and barred the only two doors into the house, but I think anyone or – thing could still get in easily. If only Blas were here. Nana said he has been protecting me. Then where is he?

The storm seems to have passed. At least the wind is no longer blowing. The wolves have started to howl again. Why? What does it mean? Does it mean anything or nothing? I have heard wolves howl before they go on a hunt as if to call the pack together. What about werewolves? Werewolves only come out during a full moon and then only at night. But if Vlad is a werewolf that is not the case. Or is it? Silver is supposed to be a protection against werewolves. Only something silver, a knife, a spear, a bullet can kill them. Silver. Is that what Nana meant? The silver cross would protect me against him? Is that why she said never to take it off?

What is happening now? Suddenly the wolves have stopped howling. No! I know he is out there. I can feel his yellow eyes staring at me. He is there. He is sitting in the middle of a semi-circle of wolves. He is much larger than all the rest. Black – huge.

Dear God! What am I going to do now? I know this is Vlad. It has to be. He has gotten up, stretched and yawned, showing huge white fangs. It's as if he knows nothing can stop him and he is confident in his power. Now he is moving towards me slowly, deliberately, his eyes fixed and staring.

Oh God! What is happening now? He has stopped halfway across the clearing and turned his head. He has gone very still, the ruff around his neck standing out. His tail has become rigid curling up behind him. Oh! I see. Another huge black wolf has come in sight moving fast. Its lips curled in a snarl.

The two wolves circle each other stiff legged. The one lunges. Fangs flashing they feint, seeking an advantage. First one, then the other shows wounds. In the dim light from the stars I can't tell which is which. They metamorphose together from wolf to human never staying in one form for long. The snow around them has turned red. Finally one takes advantage of an opening and sinks his fangs in the throat of the other. One lies still on the red snow while the other stands over him. He raises his head to the sky and lets out a long triumphant howl. Then the wolf slowly changes into human form and starts to turn towards me.

But which one? Blas or Vlad? Dear God! Which one?

Biography of
Dr. Alden B. Hall

Born in Burlington, Vermont, Alden Hall lived in Newton, New Jersey for thirty-five years before moving to The Villages. He earned his B.A. from Princeton University New Jersey, his M.A. from Amherst College Massachusetts, and his M.D. from Rochester University New York. Dr. Hall held life and death in his hands as a practicing surgeon from 1961 thru 1993 and as Medical Director from 1985 thru 1995. Alden and wife Monica are the parents of a daughter and two sons. He began to write in The Villages in 2001 to keep his mind agile and supple. In a series of memoirs he described his life as a surgeon. *A Funny Thing Happened on the Way to the O.R.* is a collection of pieces drawn from those stories. His first completed work was a mystery novel and he is currently working on memoirs of his life as draftee in the army.

Dr. Alden Hall, one of the Creative Writer's Group favorite authors, has managed to keep his fellow writers laughing until their sides hurt as he regales them with stories entitled *"A Funny Thing Happened On The Way to the O R."*

A FUNNY THING HAPPENED ON THE WAY TO THE O.R.

Memoir

by Alden B. Hall, M.D.

In the 1960's my associates and I became very busy as our medical practice expanded. So much so, that an associate held evening office hours twice a week. One evening, he received a call for a house-visit. He explained that he had late office hours and that it would be awhile before he could make the call.

"That's okay, doc. We'll leave the light on for you. Come when you can."

He finished office hours at nine-thirty. He got his bag, removing his white coat, put on his suit coat, got in his car and drove seven miles to the farm house.

When he got there, the house was dark except for a weak light coming through the transom over the front door. He took his bag, and started up the walk toward the door in the pitch darkness. Suddenly, he found himself falling to the bottom of a large hole. Wet dirt was all around him. He gathered himself, slung his bag over the edge of the pit, and clambered up the four foot climb.

He reached the top, found his bag in the dark. He realized he was covered with wet dirt, but he nevertheless warily proceeded to the door and knocked. No answer. He continued pounding on the door, not being in the best humor. The door eventually opened and the farmer stood there in his pajamas.

"We thought you weren't coming when it got so late, so we went to bed," the farmer said.

Then he saw the dirt-covered doctor standing there with mud all over his suit, shirt, and tie, as well as his shoes.

"You have a hole in your sidewalk – I couldn't see it in the dark, and fell in!"

"We're putting in a new septic tank," said the farmer, who realized he might be liable should the doctor decide to raise a legal fuss about it. Fearing the worst he invited him in, doing his best to get the mud off.

The associate wanted only to complete his call, go home and get into a hot shower. The patient, the farmer's wife, suddenly became well, and didn't need a doctor's visit after all.

When my associate finally left the house, carefully avoiding the gaping canyon in the walk, he literally knew of the pitfalls of house calls.

Medical language has always been a problem when dealing with patients. They try hard to use the correct medical terms, but often come up with words that are painful to the doctor's ears, – "menestrating" instead of "menstruating," "prostrate" instead of "prostate," "larnyx" instead of "larynx," and "vomicking" instead of "vomiting," and so on. Doctors get used to such travesties, but still shudder at some of them.

We were instructed throughout medical school to avoid medical terms while explaining things to patients because they often misinterpret what is told them unless one is very careful. An example was given us by our pharmacology instructor:

A patient, an old farmer with a bad case of hemorrhoids, visited his doctor. The doctor carefully instructed the patient about sitz baths and gave him several suppositories to use, saying, "Put one of these in your rectum after each sitz bath."

The patient went home, took a sitz bath and then asked his wife, "Do we have a rectum around the house?"

His wife said, "No, but we do have that old pump organ in the parlor." They agreed that would have to do.

After each sitz bath, he dutifully put a suppository in the pump organ.

At the end of the week, he returned to the doctor.

"Are you feeling better?" he was asked.

"Not much!" replied the patient.

"Did you use the suppositories?" asked the doctor.

"Doc, for all the good they did me, I might as well have shoved them up my ass!"

While that story may be apocryphal, it pointed out that such things do happen in reality.

My associate had a patient who was very excitable, bordering on manic-depression. He wrote a prescription for a calmative, but the woman said she couldn't afford it at the time, so he gave her some sample suppositories to use in place of the pills. He carefully told her to be sure to remove all of the wrapping before use.

At the end of the day, he got a phone call from the patient's husband, complaining that his wife was "having a hell of a time swallowing the damn things."

Accents can be equally confusing. For example, during a class in pharmacology a prominent cardiologist of Chinese extraction was lecturing on the effects of certain medications on the pulse rate and rhythm of the heart – the following exchange occurred:

"If you give adrenalin, the *Blupeshaw* go up," stated our prof. "If you give diuretic, the *Blupeshaw* go down."

None of us knew what he was talking about. One of the students asked him, saying he didn't quite get the word that went "up or down" with the medication.

"*Blupeshaw! Blupeshaw!* B-L-O-O-D P-R-E-S-S-U-R-E! – *Blupeshaw*."

We all heaved a collective sigh of relief!

Even now, when I put the cuff on the patient's arm, I think I am measuring the systolic and diastolic *Blupeshaw!*

The practice of medicine isn't all work and no play. In the early '70's, I was invited by a friend and colleague, from Sloan-Kettering Hospital in New York City, to attend a group seminar on "Radiation Oncology" to be held in Mexico City. He knew several surgeons who had trained at Sloan-Kettering who were now practicing in Mexico City.

We arrived one late afternoon at the Maria Isabella Sheraton Hotel in down town Mexico City. Several of our visiting group – all from Sloan-Kettering – were insistent on going to a "typical Mexican restaurant" for dinner. A member of the group had learned the name of one such establishment from a previous visitor to Mexico. It was called "La Plaza de la Recuerda."

After we had settled in, all sixteen of us met in front of the hotel at eight o'clock. Not knowing where "La Plaza de la Recuerda" was, we decided to take taxis. With our large crowd, this meant a minimum of four taxis. The doorman succeeded in rounding up this many – much to the delight of all four taxi-drivers – to drive the 'Yankees' to the restaurant.

My wife and I were in the lead cab with my colleague. "La Plaza de la Recuerda" we said.

"Oh, si, senor!" he seemed to gloat!

We left the hotel on the corner of the main drag, turned right at the corner, drove past the side of the hotel, turned right at the next street and stopped directly behind the hotel. Right across the street was "La Plaza de la Recuerda," with a bright neon sign announcing its presence! Had we walked out the back entrance of the hotel, we would have been there!

The cab drivers all collected their fares with wide smiles – they had caught the "gringos" again!

Inside the restaurant, it certainly was "authentic Mexican." Small tables covered in red and white checkered tablecloths, with blue cloth napkins. A half-burned candle stuck in a bottle with wax dripping down the side, sat on each table. Although the chairs were wooden, they were comfortable. We split into groups of four, and nearly filled the place.

We were handed very large menus – all in Spanish. None of us had the foggiest idea of what was available from this huge "carte." I noticed a striking young couple across the room who were obviously enjoying their meal, which, from where I sat, appeared to be a large tureen of soup. I asked our waiter in my faltering espanol, "que es esto?" pointing at the dish.

"Ah, senor, es fiesta de los pescadores."

I knew pretty much what that meant – we would call it "bouillabaisse" here in the U.S. We ordered it, along with some Mexican Beer – "La Batt" if I recall correctly. My table colleagues thought it also looked good, and ordered it, too,.

After we had a glass of beer, the waiter appeared with *four* big tureens of the "fisherman's feast," and put one in front of each of us! They were no small tureens either! There was enough seafood in each one to choke a horse! There was no way any of us could eat that much! Thankfully, the table next to us hadn't ordered, so we gratefully gave them two tureens for them to split among the four of them – as we ourselves did! We had been "had" again – one more laugh on the "gringos!"

As we ate, several men came in and went to the front of the place, produced musical instruments – two guitars, a flute and a strange-looking little harp, the likes of which I had never seen – and started to play a succession of delightful music.

We had a good time listening and downing our seafood and beer. By the time we had finished, none of us were able to handle any more of either. After settling up our bill, we walked across the street to the hotel.

The next day, we were fortunate to have tickets to the "Ballet Folklorico de Mexico." Our seats were excellent – way down front in an old opera house. Much to our surprise and delight, there, on the stage appeared the whole group from La Plaza de la Recuerda who had serenaded us the night before! This time, they didn't "get" the gringos, we really enjoyed the Mexican Folklorico Ballet.

Back in the States, my friend Joe S., a pediatrician, was used to getting phone calls from many a mother about her child's well being. There was one mother who didn't hesitate to call Joe about anything – anytime her baby did or didn't do something. Joe, being a rather phlegmatic man, took all of this without becoming perturbed.

One night, Joe's phone rang at three a.m., waking him up. It was the same young mother on the line.

"Doctor, why can't I feed my baby strained spinach?" she asked.

Joe, incredulous at such a question at that hour said, "Whaaat?"

"Why can't I feed my baby strained spinach?"

Joe, now fully awake, said, "My dear lady, it's three o'clock in the morning. Why are you calling me *now* with this question?"

"Well, all of the other mothers I know are feeding their babies strained spinach, and I wondered why I couldn't. I was lying here thinking and worrying about it, so I had to call to find out."

Joe heaved a sigh, knowing her baby to be a robust, healthy infant, and as such was practically indestructible, said, "Okay, give it a try, but not too much strained spinach the first time."

He hung up and went back to sleep.

The next evening, he set his alarm for three a.m., awoke, and called the young mother back.

"How did it go?" he asked when she finally answered.

"How did what go? Who is this?" she asked.

After identifying himself, he asked again, "How did it go? I mean feeding the baby strained spinach?"

"Doctor, it's three o'clock in the morning! Why are you calling me now?" she asked.

"I was lying here thinking and worrying about it, so I just had to call to find out!"

Apparently the strained spinach went well, because Joe never got a late-night call again from that mother.

Late in my career, I was honored by an appointment to the Judicial Council of the State Medical Society. The council was more of an arbitration group than a legal entity with corrective powers. We listened to various disputes, most of them concerned with excessive fees that some physicians charged. Nearly all of these involved a physician who valued his own services well above those of his peers – an ego trip, if you will. Nearly all were settled after hearing both sides, then getting them together to reach a reasonable settlement.

We had no legal authority to discipline anyone. If we felt there was some breach of ethics or non-professional conduct, we were obliged to refer the matter to the State Board of Medical Examiners, who had the power to suspend or revoke a doctor's license, impose fines, demand further education, and other punitive means.

Our council rarely adjudicated cases needing further referral, but at times, it came close.

One such case was sent to us by the local county judicial council, who wanted no part in it. I will try to be brief in summary as it came to us.

A pediatrician who had been in practice several years and was well established and had a good reputation in his community, was out to dinner with his family one evening. He was paged during his meal, and called his answering service. He was given the patient's number and called right then.

The patient's mother told the doctor that her toddler had a high fever and was very restless and agitated. The doctor told the mother that he would stop on his way home and see the child.

When he arrived it was about eight o'clock. His examination revealed that the child had one of those exanthems so common at that age. They are self limited and last only two or three days. The only concern with such illnesses is the fever accompanying them. If the temperature rises too high there is a danger of febrile convulsions. The only treatment, therefore, is to control the child's temperature.

The most effective treatment is aspirin. The pediatrician was also aware that high doses of aspirin could lead to complications – the worst being Reyes' Syndrome. He therefore elected to give the child spread-out doses of infant aspirin. He left six doses after giving the patient the initial dose. He instructed the mother as follows:

"Check the temperature in an hour. If it's still elevated, give him another dose. Then check his temperature every two hours. Give another dose each time if his temperature is still up!"

The mother seemed to understand this, and the doctor went home to bed.

Later, the phone rang. It was the young mother. "His temperature is down to one hundred and three degrees. Should I give him another dose?" The doctor responded patiently that, yes, she should – as she was instructed to do. The pediatrician tried to go to sleep. At eleven, she called again. "His temperature is down to one hundred and two degrees. Should I give him the next dose?" The doctor again patiently instructed her as to what to do.

The phone rang again at one o'clock, three o'clock, five o'clock. Each time the temperature was subsiding nicely, but each time she asked about giving the next dose.

Each time, she was told to give the dose – as long as there was fever. By seven o'clock in the morning, the pediatrician had had little to no sleep, and was upset that this mother just couldn't or wouldn't follow his simple instructions.

At seven o'clock, she again phoned, "His temperature is normal and he's sound asleep," she said. "I have one more dose of aspirin left over. What shall I do with it?"

By now the doctor was out of sorts, angry and frustrated, so he told her in no uncertain terms *just what she could do with it!*

The mother was aghast at this outburst, and they slammed down their phones simultaneously.

She was so angry that she called her lawyer, who advised her correctly to report him to the Medical Society. This she did, and was referred to the county society – who sent her complaint to the judicial council of the county society. This August body wouldn't touch it with a ten-foot pole and promptly bounced the case to the state council. We were obliged to hear it.

"Due process" means both parties must be heard and given the latitude to present each side. We arranged for both the mother and doctor to appear the same day. The mother told us her side of the case – pretty much as outlined above. We asked her to wait, then heard the doctor's side – again as outlined. He admitted he had lost his temper and with it, his self-control. He was obviously regretful about the situation.

We called the mother back in and told her that the doctor had confirmed her story, and was sorry about it. Did she want to pursue a charge of unprofessional conduct? There was no question that it was exactly that! The doctor had admitted it.

We explained that this case would have to go to the Board of Medical Examiners. They could, if they found the charge serious enough, revoke or suspend his license to practice medicine.

She replied: "Do you mean he can't be my pediatrician any more? Who will take care of my children? I want him to be my kid's doctor!"

We suggested that the two of them meet and talk it over. She went into the little office where the doctor was awaiting our decision. They stayed for almost a half-an-hour, while the council bit its collective finger nails.

Finally, they emerged, both of them smiling, but both wiping tears from their eyes. They left arm-in-arm, and the Council had scored another victory and I had another example of the many unforseen, but intriguing events that awaited me in my life as a doctor.

Biography of
Jon David Douglas

Midwest born (Iowa) Jon David Douglas, studied speech and dramatic arts, as well as creative writing at the University of Iowa, known for its famous Writer's Workshop. He received a degree in Sociology and Anthropology from Iowa, but decided after graduation to pursue a career in radio, television and film. Starting out as a radio copywriter, he soon became program director of the station, later working for a leading New York advertising agency as broadcast director. Jon David then moved into television writing and production and worked for two major networks. Most recently, he's been a writer-producer with the giant television retailer, Home Shopping Network (HSN), in Tampa Bay, Florida.

When medical reasons made it impossible to continue his broadcast career, Jon David decided to concentrate his talents on fiction writing, a dream he'd held for many years. Douglas now lives in Central Florida where he continues to write daily. *Who Am I?*, the working title of a novel in progress, was suggested by the author's own dilemma of nearly total amnesia. He is the author of two published novels, *CODY, a Boy's Odyssey*, (2003) and *A Place Out of Time* (2004). Both books are available at local bookstores or on-order from most Internet Book Services.

WHO AM I?

Fiction

by Jon David Douglas

CHAPTER 1

The man was lying face down on bricks in an alley. He raised his head a little and was startled to look directly into the furry face of a cat. He had never seen a cat's face so close before and at this distance it seemed huge. The cat looked directly into his eyes, only inches away. He saw the cat's golden flecked irises with the narrow black slits of the pupils in the center. Whiskers radiated out from the pink nose. It's face was scarred and the black and white coat matted with clumps of grease, dirt and dried blood.

The cat warily sniffed at the man's head, then closed its eyes and sneezed suddenly. The man wiped the moist spray from his face with his hand. He looked beyond the scraggily cat to the entrance of the alley. It was early morning, for there were thin curls of wispy haze typically seen right after dawn when the nighttime temperatures drop sharply during a warm humid spell.

What time was it, anyway? He glanced for the watch on his wrist, but it was gone. He reached for his wallet, but that, too, was gone, his back pocket empty. He felt naked with the discovery. Fear shot through him and there was a pounding in his head, a headache like none he'd ever felt before. It seemed to hurt with increased intensity, the more he concentrated on it. It just got worse and worse. His hand went to his head and he felt something hard, yet semi-sticky. When he looked at his hand he saw that there was blood on his fingertips.

What had happened? He tried to think back, but nothing would come to memory. He noticed the cat continuing to skulk about and he vaguely remembered walking though the alley. Then even that faded. The more he concentrated, the further away the memory seemed to become. He panicked. *Where was he? Where had he been? Where was he going?* He tried again to remember, but couldn't. He felt another stab of fear and his stomach tightened into a knot. He took a deep breath, closing his eyes in an effort to think more clearly, then promptly passed out.

He slowly came to, into a state of dazed awareness, as someone was going through his pockets. It was full daylight as he willed himself back to complete consciousness, he could see thick rubber wheels as he blinked to clear his vision. Moving just his eyes, he looked up, noting the rusty chrome of a supermarket cart. It was filled with assorted junk and bulky black garbage bags. To his right he saw a pair of dirty scuffed tennis-type shoes with legs emerging from them. The legs wore sagging stockings with runs, above that a ragged blue gingham dress and a dirty faded brown coat buttoned with the one remaining button. Where the coat hung open he saw a gray sweater over a pink sweater. He squinted in the sunlight, and looked into the face of an old woman.

The face was not unpleasant, but it was deeply etched with hard lines. The wrinkled face was dirty, her mouth in a toothless grin, the whole face wreathed with wispy gray hair. Lively blue eyes dominated the weathered features. As she methodically checked his pockets, the old woman – who he thought was probably a street person – hummed tunelessly to herself.

"Help me," he croaked hoarsely.

Startled, the old woman jumped back.

"Honest, I wasn't doin' nothin' wrong," she said. "I was just acheckin' to see if I could find out who you was. Yer in a bad way. At first I thought ya was just drunk, then I seen that someone has hit ya pretty hard on the head with this big board, and dropped it over here," she picked up the bloodstained two by four.

"No wonder my head hurts, so."

"Yeah, lookie at all the blood," she turned the board this way and that. "At least I imagines this to be yer blood. You've got a pretty mean gash on your head. I tried to wake ya up, but yer lights was out," she leaned near him, her breath awful as she spoke, but he supposed his was probably just as bad, judging from the disagreeable taste he had in his mouth.

"Yer head's stopped bleeding. They hit ya, then they musta took yer billfold. I mean, I didn't find nothing valuable in yer pockets. By the way, who is you?"

"I don't know!" He struggled to get up. "I just realized, I don't have the foggiest idea who I am!"

The woman looked at him quizzically. He appeared to be in his middle thirties. The man had pleasant features and was probably good-looking if he was cleaned up a little. He had sandy colored hair where it wasn't all covered with blood, his skin was evenly tanned as though frequently in the sun. He had on good clothes and expensive dress shoes, although they were smudged with alley dirt.

"Ya must *be somebody*," she said as she put down the blood-stained board. "Yer dressed important."

He tried to get up again. She offered her arm and he struggled to his feet. He reeled as if coming out of a hangover, staggering when he tried to walk. He felt a little sick to his stomach.

"You'd better jist sit yerself down a spell." She pulled a wooden crate out from others in a nearby pile of trash. "I think it's sturdy enough, if you don't sit too hard."

Who am I, where am I supposed to be going and where do I belong? he thought. "God, it's frightening to be so confused," he said. Holding his head with his hands, he tried to stop the dizziness. He felt ice cold even though he was sweating profusely beneath his suit coat. There was a racket of whirs and grinding. He turned toward the sound and saw that a garbage truck and crew had entered the alley.

"Oh damn it all! he said. "I wanted to look in all the trash cans around here to see if my billfold had been tossed into one of them, and now the garbage truck is coming and I won't have time."

"I looked in all the cans afore I found you. If it was in any of them I would have found it, believe me." She waved her hand toward her jam-packed shopping cart. "I scrounge in all the cans nearly everyday, and I save anything I think might be worth something, I wouldn't have missed or overlooked it. We just need to look in the ones at the end where I haven't been yet. Let's go."

She began pushing the cart down the alley. He followed unsteadily.

"Where are we?" he asked.

"In an alley off State Street."

"No, I mean *where*, what city?"

"Oh, ya mean ya don't even know what town yer in?"

"No, please tell me for Gods sake!"

"We're in Albany."

"Albany?"

"Yes, Albany, the state capital of New York."

"I know that. But, what am *I* doing here? I don't think I know anyone in Albany."

"Don't ya recognize nothing?"

"Only thing I can remember, *sort of*, is a large black and white cat."

"Oh, you've seen Black and Whitey. I haven't seen him for a week. But he usually hangs around these parts. Anyway I always sees him here. Try hard to remember yer name agin, sweetie."

"That's just it. I still can't remember. I used to know it, though. I know I did."

"Ya can't remember yer name, I never heard of such a thing."

"Damn it, I know I must have a name, but I just can't think what it is. Hell, even the cats's got a name. What time is it? No, tell me what day, what year it is?"

"The woman rummaged through her junk and came up with an old wind-up clock. "It's twenty minutes after the hour," she said holding it to her ear. "I can't tell you what hour, because the little hand's gone."

"Oh, that's great."

"Well, I reckon it's before nine, 'cus of the garbage truck and all. They usually git off the streets before nine. So it must be about eight – twenty. It's June fifth, I think, I really don't know, because I don't keep track of days, ya see. One day's just like another, but I happen to know it's Thursday because I've got to check in with county welfare tomorrow, that's always on Friday."

She told him the year. He stared at her in shock, closed his eyes and shook his head as if trying to clear the cobwebs from his brain.

"I thought this was the '80s."

"Oh boy, don't I wish," she said, chuckling, "I was a lot younger then."

The garbage truck came nearer.

"We'd better hurry if we're gonna look in all the cans. Once the garbage people took my cart thinking *it* was trash."

"Well, isn't it, mostly?"

"Not to me it isn't. If I leaves it anywhere, peoples steal it, so it must be worth something. It's got all my belongings. Maybe it's not worth much, but to me it's everything I own."

"I'm sure it has great value to you."

"Lookie at this radio. When I have money for batteries it plays wonderful. Even Beethoven. If that isn't living, I don't know what is. Let's keep looking."

They checked more of the trash cans finding no wallet, although the woman pounced upon several items she apparently prized, carrying them carefully to her cart.

"You must enjoy finding things you like," said the man, resting again on a box.

"Talk about recycling. Us street people were the first recyclers. Ya hear a lot about it now, I read about it almost every day in the newspapers, but we been doin' it even before it was the thing to do. We live off of everything recycled, even food. We could teach people a thing or two about waste."

"Maybe you could find some hot coffee? That would taste mighty good right about now."

"That's one thing ya jist can't find in garbage, hot coffee – cans of soda sometimes, or maybe half full jars of instant coffee, but then, where do ya get the hot water?

"A restroom?"

"The water coming out of restroom facets isn't hot enough. We can get coffee at a fast-food place in the next block, if you want some. Do you think you'll be able to walk a piece now?"

He got up and walked a few steps uncertainly. He steadied himself and walked up and down the alley slowly.

"Yer walking better. Find anything that I missed in yer pockets? I didn't find nothin, but I didn't go deep."

He put his hands in his pockets. "Wait, here's something – darn, it's just keys . . . but to what, I wonder? My car, maybe my home – wherever that is."

"Oh, never ya mind, we'd better jist keep looking."

But they had no luck finding anything in the remaining trash cans.

"Nothing." she said.

"Oh hell, I guess it's not here," he said.

"The guy what hit ya either's still got yer wallet, or he threw it somewhere else. We might jist as well go for coffee now."

"Yeah."

She put her arm around him to hold him upright, and at first he was embarrassed to walk with the old woman's arm around him. Then he thought, *I really don't know anyone. So, what the hell, I've got bigger things to worry about.*

"We'll drink our coffee at that park bench over there," she pointed to a small pocket park across the street from McDonald's. There was a colorful mural on the wall behind the bench.

Pointing to the picture she said, "That represent's the history of the area, the Erie canal that comes through here. The building with the smokestack is to remind us of all the old clothing mills and factories that used to be here."

"What about the lightbulb?"

"The lightbulb symbolizes the big General Electric factory near here. Edison was all part of that, back about 85 years? You've heard tell of Edison, didn'tcha?"

"Yeah, I know about Edison – I just didn't know he was around here that much."

"He musta been. Now you just wait here, look at the picture and watch my cart while I go get the coffee. How do ya like yer coffee?"

"I don't know. I guess black."

"Maybe ya want sugar today for energy, it's free ya know."

"Okay, with sugar."

While he waited, he decided to look through her possessions, just to be certain the billfold wasn't among them. *It's a virtual department store,* he thought In addition to the purses, table lamp with no shade and radio – boom box, she had a doll with a missing leg, more sweaters, worn-out shoes, various half-used cosmetics, unopened canned goods, cereal boxes, several books, a portable typewriter and finally cigar boxes secured with rubber bands. He peeked inside to see what the boxes contained – only cheap jewelry – no wallet. Surprisingly, the realization that it wasn't there made him happy, although he'd give anything to find it somewhere. He carefully put her treasurers back exactly the way he'd found them.

He glanced toward McDonalds. She crossed the street carrying two styrofoam cups.

"Careful, it's hot." She handed one cup to him. "I hope ya like the sugar, I put in a lot."

He removed the plastic cover, and took a sip. It was hot, and much, much too sweet for his taste. "I guess I like it black," he said. "But it's okay for now. By the way, what's your name?"

"Mary."

"Mary, thanks, I needed a jolt that caffeine and lots of sugar will give. Pay you when I can."

"Don't worry yerself none. I get $500 a month. I know what its like to be alone, hurting and needing."

"Well, anyway thanks."

"When yer done with yer coffee we'll head over to the free clinic and see if they can fix you up. At least clean ya up and slap a bandage on yer head. Don't hurry none . . . Ya gotta have some name, so I'm gonna call ya Ben, one of my best husbands had that name, and I liked it . . . Ben," she repeated and smiled at him. How do you like the name, Ben?"

"Well, I'm pretty certain Ben isn't my real name, but until I find out what is, it suits me just fine It's a good name."

Several pigeons gathered near her, noticing them, she set her cup on the bench, covering it with a napkin. She turned to the cart.

"I always feeds the birds," she said taking out a cereal box.

She shook corn flakes from the half empty box onto the sidewalk and threw a handful into the air. Pigeons arrived from everywhere, even from a bank portico a block away – in essence all the pigeons from a 300 foot radius spotted the food, flew to the park and began to peck at the flakes. Some of the bolder pigeons flew to her shoulders and one even sat on her head. More of the purple colored birds joined them, resting on her outstretched arms.

"Look Ben, I'm a statue," she said assuming a pose, standing on one foot, with one hand in front of her and one hand and leg trailing behind her. The pigeons repositioned themselves to her new posture, making the strange clucking and cooing sounds that pigeons constantly make.

"Who are you supposed to be?" he asked, laughing.

"Why Venus, of course." She looked at a bird on her shoulder. "Ben, I like the birds, sometimes there's even an all-white one – a dove I think you would call it. But I don't know where Lovey Dovey is today. Probably went to visit somebody, a friend o' his somewhere. I'll bet he'll be sorry when he finds out he missed the corn flakes.

The man drank his coffee, finally putting the empty cup into a nearby trash receptacle. Mary returned to the park bench. The pigeons strutted in front of them looking for more handouts after eating every speck of the cereal from the sidewalk.

"I think there's a place for everyone and everything in this world," said Mary. "Pigeons to clean up the place, and me to give them what I find and keeping things from going to waste. I feed Black and Whitey too, every once in a while – although he does a pretty good job of taking care of hisself. He catches mice – rats, too, if they're not too big and even go after these pigeons if I don't chase him away afore I feed 'em. All God's creatures got a place in his world – you too, we jus gotta find out what it is." She swallowed the rest of her coffee, handing him the empty cup.

"Jus throw this away for me, will you? Okay. Ready to rock and roll? The clinic's on Ferry Street, down by the Hudson River, it's not too far and it's early enough so there won't be many people there now. Sometimes it seems ya could sit there for hours waiting. While you're waiting, ya see other people bleeding and leaking blood from stab wounds. They just sits there until someone takes 'em. Nobody's got any money. You look like you gots money, but I knows you don't. See how fast you can become one of us homeless persons? Yesterday ya wasn't, now overnight you is."

"I was thinking the same thing," he said.

They walked to Ferry Street heading to a large modern building made of poured concrete. A giant red-cross was painted on the plate glass window.

"Lot's of people think this is the Red Cross, but it ain't. The big red cross is for people who can't read. It's for emergencies and poor people, operated by the Albany Medical Center near here – guess they like to practice doctoring on people who don't matter. Like the barber college. If you get a bad haircut, it's just too bad.

"I guess they have to practice on *someone*," he said.

"Never you mind, some of them young doctors is more caring for free than the old-time doctors I had to pay for, when I used to get boils and things, you know. I ain't never been to the hospital. I don't like hospitals – because that's where they keep all the sick people. I've heard of more people carried out feet first, than walking out alive."

"A hospital is kind of a last chance place, I suppose," said the man.

"One thing about Albany Medical Center – if you need medicine, they give ya free pills. Everything's free – jist a lot of red tape . . . but all I've got is time, so it's okay."

CHAPTER 2

Mary pushed her cart right into the waiting room and parked it by a row of empty seats, "You have to talk with the mean lady at the desk," she nodded toward the woman.

The man walked to the check-in desk. The receptionist was on the telephone. She was apparently talking with a friend and made no attempt to end her conversation, it seemed. While he waited, he looked about the waiting room. There were perhaps forty modern molded plastic seats. About ten seats were filled: a mother with three young children at her side and one in her arms, several older men, a boy with a bandage over his eye, and two pregnant women. A planter in the center of the waiting room was filled with green plastic plants as well as a one-time live plant, now wilted and dead.

"Name?" asked the woman, after she finally hung up the phone, hands poised over her computer keyboard. Her condescending smile irritated him.

"That's just it, I don't know what it is," he said, with an exaggerated smile back at her.

"Well, we simply have to have a name for our records," she snapped and smiled again sweetly.

"Okay, try Ben" he said.

"Ben . . . what?"

"Sorry, I don't know the last name."

"But Ben is your first name?"

"No, I just said that because you said you needed a name. Someone called me that this morning."

"But, it's not your name?"

"No, I don't think so."

"Then I'll have to change this, I'll have to enter you as a John Doe. Just like an unidentified body. You'll have to use that name whenever you come here for treatment," she said, smiling broadly. Social security number?"

"If I don't know my name, how am I going to recall my social security number?"

"Have you looked in your billfold?"

"That's just it, it was stolen."

"Then you don't have any money?" You're indigent, too?"

"Yes," he said, feeling humiliated.

"Well, we'll state that your number is unknown. You have to fill out this paper with financial information and your medical history on the back. We have to enter it all into the computer system. It's strange that you don't remember your social security number. Most people memorize it and never forget it."

"Well, I forgot it and I don't have any knowledge about any medical history either. Can't I just see a doctor?"

"First, fill out the form, and then we'll let you see a doctor. You can't pay anything?" She scrutinized him suspiciously.

"No. I don't have a cent. I just told you my wallet was taken, and you can see I need help. I got hit on the head."

"Yes, I see you've been bleeding. Do you have any pain?"

"Of course I'm in pain."

"Well, go sit down and fill out this form first to the best of your knowledge. We can't do anything without it. Then bring it back to me. Don't forget to sign it."

"As John Doe?"

"If that's the name you're using."

He sat next to Mary and looked at the form. He left the address blank, gave the rest of the information as N. A., and checked "?" on all the diseases. He signed the form with an X and wrote the name, John Doe, walked back to the receptionist and handed her the form.

"I'm sorry, but that name has been taken. It'll have to be John Doe18."

"Okay, I guess. Whatever. Just so I can see a doctor."

"What will you be treated for today, Mr. Doe?"

"What do you think? I've shown you the gash on my head. See the blood? And I must have amnesia. So I think I need a doctor for my head."

"Oh, a neurologist . . . well, then it will take some time. Maybe quite a while. Have a seat, Mr. Doe, and you'll be called when he arrives."

A little girl who had been sitting with her mother ran about the room, played near the planter and finally came over to stare at his head. She asked, "Geez, what happened to you mister? What's your name?"

"I don't know," he said. "What's yours?"

"I don't know either." She had a runny nose, a dirty face and a food-stained dress. She smiled innocently, unafraid, frank and curious.

"Lucy, don't bother the man, git back here," commanded the mother with the infant.

"Oh, yeah, now I remember, my name's Lucy," she said, then hurried back to her mother.

It seemed an endless wait, most of the other persons were called, had seen the doctor and left, including the little girl and her mother, her other brothers and sisters. Finally he was summoned.

"John Doe18."

He got up and followed the nurse in the door which led, he assumed, to the treatment areas. He was ushered into an examining room. The nurse took his vital signs, noting the numbers on a sheet which she put in his folder.

"We don't have a base line to compare these against, I'm afraid. Let's see. You have a nasty gash, the doctor will want to give you a couple of stitches. I'll clean the area."

She took gauze with some sort of liquid, he supposed alcohol and touched gently at his wound. The gauze became bloodstained and he could feel the sting of the antiseptic.

"Wow, I can feel that."

"Sorry, but it has to be cleaned. I'll have to shave a small area where the doctor will put the stitches. You'll have a little bald patch."

"Where is he?"

"The doctor's en route. He called in on his cellular phone a few minutes ago that he was leaving the hospital. Just relax. It shouldn't be much longer." She went out of the room, putting his file folder in a holder beside the door.

He sat on the examining table agonizing over the long wait, when the door abruptly opened and a man in a white lab jacket came in.

"I'm Doctor Jamison," he said. "They thought I should see you. Which is why you had to wait so long. I was doing my morning rounds when they called, but I got here as soon as I could." He held the file folder. "What seems to be the matter?" He checked the folder, "er . . . John, is it?"

"My name isn't really John, at least I don't think it is. Last night I was mugged, hit over the head pretty hard and robbed. I can't remember anything else . . . who I am or where I was going. It's kind of unnerving."

"Sometimes with a trauma to the head there is temporary amnesia. We can't be certain how long, but normally things will slowly return to your memory as the swelling goes down. It's important to remain calm."

"I don't know what to do next."

"This should be reported to the police. I'll go ahead, an' file the matter with the police. I'm bound by state law to report all acts of violence that I'm aware of."

"I see."

"The police will want to talk with you for details. They'll probably see you when I send you over to Albany Medical Center."

"I didn't know I was to be admitted."

"We want to see inside your head. There's the slight danger that your injury could be more involved than we can determine at this point."

"That's not encouraging."

"Better to be safe. You might have a skull fracture or concussion." The doctor looked at the wound. He checked his reflexes.

"What do you think, Doctor?"

"Well, all indications look good. You don't seem to have any motor function interruption. Now, I'm going to put a couple of stitches in your scalp. You'll always have a small scar there, but we need to minimize it. The reason I'm sending you to Albany Medical is because I'd like to do a Cat scan and an MRI to detect the extent of the brain injury. The amnesia is no doubt from the blow to the skull. It could be temporary or it might last for some time. We need to know the extent of the injury."

"I guess that's okay."

"Then we'll do the Cat Scan today and some psychological evaluation. I'll know better tomorrow about the availability of the MRI. I'm only allowed so many per month for the free clinic. A matter of budgeting and efficient utilization of that expensive piece of equipment. We'll try to get you up and out of the hospital as soon as possible."

"That's okay. I guess I'm not going anywhere. No important meetings I know of."

"Good," the doctor chuckled. "You seem to have a sense of humor. That's a good sign of advanced brain activity. Now let's do the stitches."

The doctor put in the stitches, the patient winced slightly during the procedure.

"There now, that wasn't so bad was it?"

"No." He felt his scalp where the stitches were.

"Better not touch it. You'll start the bleeding again."

"It doesn't hurt now. Of course your anesthetic is working fully, now that you're done."

"Sorry about that. In a week we'll take the stitches out."

"A week?"

"Will you remember?"

"Maybe you'd better write me a note."

The doctor wrote the note on a prescription blank. "Okay, here's your note." He handed it to the man, now straining to see the stitches in the wall mirror.

"You sew pretty nice, doc."

"Reminds me of some stitches I did once on a fishing trip. My friend cut himself deeply with his fishing knife," the doctor recalled. "I had to sew him up with fish line. Only thing we had – luckily I had a needle in the first aid kit. We used Old Grand Dad for antiseptic as well as anesthetic. My pal was feeling no pain, but I couldn't get him to quit singing. I think he suffered more from the hangover than from the pain of the cut and the stitches."

"How do I get to the hospital? Do I walk? Is it a long way?"

"It's several miles. I'm heading back in a few minutes, so I'll take you. You've got your note, any other questions?"

"You seem pretty knowledgeable about amnesia. I suppose you've seen memory loss before?"

"Quite often. It's my speciality, but every case is a little different."

"How's that?"

"Well some memory losses come and go. Sometimes bits and pieces start coming back. Little things will trigger memory – music or even the whiff of a familiar odor. Other times it's all at once, like a great enlightenment and sometimes, unfortunately, memory never completely returns. It's hard to determine. Because we don't know, what we don't know."

"I know some things, but nothing important. For instance I know the world's highest tide takes place in the Bay of Fundy in Canada. Some 48 feet. Now, I ask you, what good is it to know that? Why is it I can remember that, but can't remember anything essential? About my life and me, personally? Is it just gone forever?"

"Sometimes partial amnesia lasts a few days, in other cases months or years. It's all still in your brain cells."

"Then why can't I see it?"

"The information is locked up in the brain somewhere, we just don't know what the triggers are to get it out."

"So you say it's all still there, waiting to come out?"

"Let me put it this way, it's like having one big file room with drawers of files about everything you know. But there are no labels on the drawers and your secretary, the one and only person who knows the unique filing system, suddenly walks out and quits on you. You may be able to find a few random things, but you're stuck until you figure out her complete filing system or until you can get her to come back to work."

"It's funny when you describe it that way, and I think I understand it a little better now."

"Sometimes it's a psychological thing, psychologically you might just want to remain in an amnesic state. Maybe you want to avoid some pressing problem or some other difficult thing in your life that's painful to remember, things you'd rather not face or think about, such as an unhappy home or the death of a loved one. There are many possibilities."

"I sure hope that's not my problem."

"Very possibly not. You may never be aware of it if it is."

"One thing I'm aware of, is the fact I have no money. I told the woman at the desk. She was kinda difficult, but didn't tell me much."

"Oh, Dorothy Buttress, yes she can be a real pain sometimes. You can guess what we call her around here. Don't worry, I'll fill out those indigent papers so the county, New York State and the Medical Center will take care of everything. Not to worry."

"I'm grateful. I couldn't imagine what to do."

"This is what medicine is supposed to be about, helping people who need help, not being in practice to get rich."

"Nice attitude."

"See, not all doctors are worrying about where their next BMW is coming from, there are a few dedicated ones around."

"Thanks doctor."

"I'll be leaving in about fifteen minutes. Go back to the waiting room and I'll come and get you to give you a ride when I'm ready to leave."

He walked back to the reception area. Mary was still there, nervously waiting for news of his examination.

"How are you, what did they say?" she asked.

"They're checking me into the hospital this morning. The doctor is going to put me through some exams. He said I might come out of my amnesia soon and then again I may not. The doctor is gonna drive me to the hospital. So if you want to leave, go ahead."

But Mary waited with him until Doctor Jamison came to take him away. She waved goodbye when he pulled away in the doctor's car.

"Bye Ben," she mouthed the words quietly as the car disappeared around the corner. He looked back at her and waved. Then he looked straight ahead. It was the beginning of the rest of his life.

Biography of
Ray Andrews

The Proud Dart, by Ray Andrews, is an example of this author's unique creativity and wonderful humor. Ray came to Florida from Wadsworth, Illinois. During his career, he worked in Chicago as an advertising executive. He is presently writing a novel about a bizarre murder that takes place in a popular Village night club. Ray has titled his story *Weaver's Sweet Revenge*. It features a bumbling detective Walter Weaver.

THE PROUD DART

Fiction

by Ray Andrews

I was one proud dart. I weighed in at 27 grams, had a tip as sharp as a sewing needle; a titanium body as sleek as a torpedo and was beautifully fletched with the snow-white wing feather of a Ferruginous Hawk.

I was two hundred and ninety-eight bucks, new. Actually, that was for the set of three of us. But old Thrower used us to make that money back, many times over.

We were pros and Thrower treated us that way. He built us a special mahogany, velvet-lined case and carved little beds for us snug enough to keep us from jouncing around going and coming to McGinty's almost every night of the week.

We did not play kiddy darts. We never used the bulls eye side of the board. We played the other side; the one that looks like twenty pieces of pizza divided by those little wire dividers.

Our game was 501 which we played for a dollar a point. Usually, there were also a bunch of side bets going on every game. Some nights, a grand could trade hands before last call. And most often, the last hand to touch that money at last call was Thrower's.

I'm proud to say I was not only part of a great team, but the anchor dart. Thrower put a little black dot on my tail so he could know it was me he was throwing last on every three-dart turn.

Thrower was twenty-eight at the time. That's the best age for a good darter. He has the experience to play smart and his hand-eye coordination is still as good as ever. And, most importantly, he wasn't married yet so he had the time to play almost every night of the week. Which, I don't care what you may have heard or read, is the only way to keep yourself on top of your game.

We'd go over to McGinty's at least four nights a week. What roaring good times we had! When Thrower walked through the door old Bobby-The-B drew his Bud Light and had it on the bar before the door closed again.

McGinty's was Thrower's home tavern. It was over on Oak Street right across from the Sears Home Improvement Center. I hear it's gone now. In fact I think they're both gone. Somebody said it's a car wash or an auto parts place now. I don't get out like I used to, so I'm not sure.

Guys used to accuse Thrower of sandbagging. You know, playing bad the first few games and then, when the stakes got right, suddenly turning on his real ability. Not true. I would know. Thrower was never that kind of guy. He was too proud. The real story is he couldn't throw darts worth a damn until about the third or fourth beer. After that, he was on after-burner. His arm would start moving like a piston in a Rolls Royce, but not until that fourth beer.

Oh, man, was he something to see. I could always feel that magic moment coming on. Suddenly, he'd be holding me light as he'd hold a baby bird. He'd line me up, eye to target and – one pump, two, three and I'd be sailing like a bullet, dead-on to the points we needed to win.

But don't get it wrong, It wasn't all Thrower. I came by my steep price tag honestly. Back then, I was in such good shape I could actually curve to the side or up or down as much as an eighth of an inch. Think about that.

It takes about as long for a dart to go from hand to target as it takes to say "Thwack!" In that short bit of time I could move a whole number over on the dart board.

I'll never forget the time when, as usual, everybody was standing on both sides of the throwing lane screaming at Thrower – whether they were rooting for him to win or to lose. Everybody yelled until you thought your head would never clear again.

Then, with that big Jackie Gleason flourish of his, he'd first chug down his draft and then carefully remove me from his left hand and nestle me down between the feathery-light fingers and thumb of his right hand. He'd level me out in front of him and sight down my body with so much concentration it made me shiver. The shouting would quiet to a murmur. Then, the room would go so quiet I could hear the beer cooler motor thunking along under the bar. He pumped his arm once, and again, and go! I was away.

I immediately realized I was sailing for the sixteen and we needed a double seven to win. The double seven was on the other side of the wire divider between the sixteen and the double seven pizza pieces. I spun clockwise, to my right, and pulled up on my nose enough to jump the wire between the slices and then the double wire, too. And Thwack! I was in!

The place went crazy.

"Bud for everyone!" Thrower cried out. Thrower was the man of the hour. And, if I must say so myself, I was the dart of the hour.

As I already said, I was Thrower's anchor dart. And, you probably already guessed that Thrower was the anchor darter on McGinty's team. Every year, for the four years Thrower had been on the team, McGinty's won the Championship in the Tri-County Bar Darts League sponsored by Thrower's favorite beer, Bud Light.

The last year in the league, the fifth for us, we again anchored McGinty's Team. We were down to the last game of the season with the championship on the line. If we beat Pairadice Inn, it was ours. If not, it was theirs. Each member of the winning team got a sterling silver beer mug engraved with the Bud Light logo and their own name, along with the date and the name of the bar.

Since we were the away team, most of the crowd was rooting against us; good-natured ribbing, except for the big betters, which come to think of it, was most everybody.

We were down to the end of the match. We needed 20 points to take the series. Thrower was on line. If he missed his sequence, Pairadice would cakewalk away with the championship. McGinty's would not even get another turn.

Thrower's first throw was a double three. The next was a six. Now all we needed was a double four. He emptied his draft and handed it to a teammate for a refill. He stepped to the line. His teammate handed him a foaming fresh one. Thrower did his Jackie Gleason and flipped the empty glass over his shoulder right into the bartender's hands.

Thrower shifted me from his left hand to his right. His touch was as light and yet as steady as I had ever felt it. He cocked his arm and sighted down the length of me from eye to board, taking dead aim on number four.

Every last person in the place stopped breathing. In the silence, I realized that the Pairadice cooler motor sounded exactly like McGinty's.

A whole year's worth of hard work and practice and drinking and competition were on the line with this one last throw. There were double stacks of side-bet money all over the bar top.

Thrower pumped once. He pumped again. One last pump and I was airborne!

I was about to relax and enjoy the ride when I saw I was going to thwack the thirteen, not the four.

I spun counter-clockwise faster than ever before in my life. As my fletches bit into the air, I felt myself start to curve to the right. With an inner smile, I closed my eyes and listened for the sweetest thwack of my life. But it was not to be.

There was a feather-rattling clink. Suddenly out of control, my tail flipped up and my body slammed broadside against the board. Before I could even cry out, I was diving head first into the empty peanut shells on the floor.

It was a million-to-one shot. I had hit the little wire between the thirteen and the four. My tip could find no cork to dig into and bounced off the board. There was no place for me to go but down.

The last thing I heard before I crunched into the peanut shells was the home bar crowd going nuts over their home bar team, the new Champions of The Tri-County Bar Darts League.

In the confusion, I called for help to get me out of those shells. But, no one could possibly hear me, I was smothered by the shells.

Then some big Pairadice oaf backed into me and kicked me with his heel so hard that he bent my tip at least twenty degrees off center. Talk about a bad night!

When Thrower finally sifted through the shells to find me, he picked me up and held me tenderly in both hands as he inspected my injury.

With all the beer he drank as well as the disappointment of losing only to see my poor broken schnoz, well, I thought he might cry.

I should have known better. Like the man he was, like the man he is, he firmly shook hands with the Pairadice team, even managing a smile when he told them how good they were. I may have been the only one to notice that his lips were smiling, but not his eyes.

The next day, Thrower locked me into his workbench vice and got to setting me right. He had the touch of a neurosurgeon. He would pry a little here, twist a little there, tap me lightly on one side and then on the other. Around and around he worked me over until my crooked little beak was a straight as new. Then he honed my nose and washed and trimmed my fletches. I felt as good as new, and I think I was.

That night, he packed us up and we headed for McGinty's. Right away, we lost two games by the worse scores ever. It didn't get better. It never got better.

At first I thought it was me, or maybe just a case of nerves after the big loss the night before. But then I noticed Thrower's touch was not as soft as before. His pumping motion was not as smooth and sure. Even after four beers. He had lost his confidence in us, which caused him to lose confidence in himself.

I felt I was flying as true as I ever had in my life, but Thrower couldn't make himself believe it. He couldn't just let the equipment do the job the way pros do, no matter what the sport. I felt him trying to steer me. His pace was off. That touch that made me an extension of his hand was missing. He never got it back. Our run had come to an end. Our championship days were over.

Then other things happened that would make it impossible to go back to what we had.

First, his cabinet-making factory made him a foreman. With his big raise came a lot of new responsibilities. He couldn't stay out all night playing darts the way you have to if you're going to be a star.

Then he met a woman who soon became Mrs. Thrower. The nights at McGinty's became fewer and fewer. Then Mrs. Thrower told Thrower it was time for a bigger house. They needed a house with another bedroom and a playroom – Junior Thrower was on the way.

So we moved out of McGinty's neighborhood to find a place with better schools.

I could see it was the end of an era. I just wish that when the team broke up it didn't have to be the way it was.

On moving day, somebody left our mahogany, velvet-lined case unlocked. On the way out to the van, the movers spilled the box. It was raining very hard and my screams for help were lost in the roar of the thunder.

My two buddies fell all the way down into the street. My last glimpse of them still haunts me late at night. The water was swirling them around closer and closer to a storm sewer. I was fortunate enough to see what was going to happen when the box spilled and was able to spin myself enough to land in Thrower's open tool kit instead of on the street.

Thrower didn't find me for a long time. When he did, he howled with laughter. I think it was with happiness. But, well, I was a sight. I was covered with three-in-one oil that had spilled into the bottom of his toolbox. Then when they carried the box into his new basement workroom, I rolled back and forth in a film of emery paper grit, so maybe he was laughing at how grungy I looked.

Either way, he spent a good ten minutes cleaning me up. Then he picked me up and pumped once, twice, three times – and hurled me into this cork message board over his worktable. He turned off the lights and clumped upstairs to watch TV with Junior and Mrs. Thrower.

It is dark down here in the basement. And so quiet I can hear all the laughter and goings-on upstairs, which usually cheers me up. I do have the water heater to keep me company, but it's simply not as jolly as McGinty's beer motor used to be. But, see? I'm holding up just fine. I'd appreciate it if you would ignore how dull my point has become. And the water heater says the patina on my body makes me look more distinguished. I think it just makes me look older. As for how my snow-white feather fletches look gray, I am sure it is just the dust down here in the basement.

Thrower drops by once in a while, usually to fix a toy or do some kind of home repair project. I like to pretend, but I don't think it is to see me.

I do remember last Christmas Eve as a fun time. Thrower came down to put together a two-wheeler for his son after the boy went to bed. Thrower used me to pin the instructions up where he could read them. See? They are still here. What I remember about that night was that he brought down a bottle of beer to sip while he worked. The smell of that beer brought back so many good memories.

Biography of
Peggy Miller

Peggy Miller writes delightful poetry, memoirs and commentaries about the oddities and treasures of present day life. Peggy was born in Rockville Center, Long Island New York. She attended Hood College and later American University. She tells us that she began writing as soon as she could read. She has published two chapbooks: Martha Contemplates The Universe (Frith Press) and Peggy Miller's Greatest Hits in the Pudding House Series. In addition, Peggy is also an Associate Editor for the Comstock Review in Syracuse, New York.

HANGING ON

Memoir

by Peggy Miller

When I went to college I lived in the girls' dormitory – no guys in the whole building. And if the plumber came or someone to move furniture, he was accompanied by the house mother who stood at the end of the hall and bellowed, "Man on the floor!" We thought that was sexy: *man* – on the – *floor*!

The house mother's name was Miss Ault. She was old, white-haired and skinny – she was also nasty! She would perform unannounced room inspections, assessing demerits for beds unmade, clothing strewn, shades raised. She referred to us as "ladies", and spewed rules.

Ladies keep a neat room.

Ladies don't cause a ruckus.

Ladies are never seen barefoot.

Ladies always wear hats with their suits on Sundays and for tea.

Ladies, stand tall!

Ladies, enough!

There were broad, dim stairwells in the dorm and on the landing just below my floor a marble pedestal on which sat a big marble bust of Minerva, goddess of education (or dignity or something like that). We tormented Minerva – propping up the janitor's mop so that it became her hair, dressing her with sunglasses, lipstick, draping her with flowery oversized dresses from the free store, giving her cigarettes. Once someone carried Minerva to the elevator and left her in it! We laughed ourselves silly!

Miss Ault always seemed to know when we were up to something. She wore sneakers, so we couldn't hear her coming, and we never knew from which direction she would appear. For any of our shenanigans we appointed a lookout, just in case!

Even so, I was nearly caught. I ran for the nearest room – door locked! Tried the next and found it open, slipped in and closed the door behind me. This was June McNally's room but she was not in – good thing. I didn't know her well and she seemed not to like me. I didn't dare leave until Miss Ault was gone, nor did I want to be caught by June – what would she think!

While I hung onto the doorknob I felt the greatest temptation – I wanted to open June's dresser drawers, peak into her closet, smell her perfume. I wanted to read her letters – look at the grades on her papers – find out what she kept under her bed! This was a dream! To be in someone else's place without her knowing, to explore all of her secrets. All my life I'd wanted to know everything about everybody. June's chiffon bedspread (which was tussled all over the bed) matched her big blue fur slippers, and her books didn't look as if she ever opened them.

Finally, after listening at the door a few more moments I took a hungry glace around, then carefully turned the doorknob and left, making my barefoot way down the hall to my own safe room.

When I was younger I used to visit Miss Russel on those long days of summer vacation. Her house, nearly strangled in its own overgrown garden, was practically devoid of modern conveniences – like Miss Russel herself.

She was in her 90's. She had neither electricity nor plumbing. Down the path from the house stood a red hand pump for water that smelled of sulfur, and further along the path a little outhouse. One concession to modern times, however, was a telephone. The postman had convinced her that she needed one in case of an emergency. Afraid of wires that might cause fires, she had the phone installed right by the front door, exactly where the wire had come through the wall.

One afternoon I walked into her house, passed the black telephone, but Miss Russel was not at home. I knew I shouldn't intrude, but my curiosity slowed my steps as I began to take my leave.

The little house was crowded – every space filled with the objects of her life. I spotted the picture of Miss Russel when she had been much younger, and still could hardly recognize her. In the photograph she stood in front of a huge wall of snow – the Blizzard of '88 she once told me, 1888.

Piled on a round table that nearly filled the room, were books of poetry, romances, eye glasses, seashells, ginger jars, penny postcards from her sister in Idaho, who was married and telling of the children's scarlet fever. Also on the table stood her kerosene lamp with its broad, milky glass and fringe of red glass beads.

And on the mantle, amidst the tea cups and daguerreotypes and candles was a picture of Miss Russel with her mother and sister when they had lived in that same house – before the garden had become so overgrown – before the house had been painted. Miss Russel had once told me that the picture was taken in the 1920's.

Then I spotted the picture of Rudolf, sporting a mustache and dressed in his best suit and ascot. The message in formal penmanship was easy to read: "All my love to Mary Alice. Just hang on until the war is over – Rudie."

But Rudie had never returned from the war. Miss Russel had told me the story, why she had remained single – an old maid – but I hadn't understood. I didn't know then there were reasons why a woman would remain single and quiet and stuck in her youth – and hang on for so many years.

Biography of
Christine Seiler

Christie Seiler has no idea what a fine writer she is. Her tales of everyday life are filled with exquisite descriptions and simply wonderful writing. Christine Davis Seiler was born in Atlanta, GA and lived there until she went to North Georgia College in Dahlonega, GA at sixteen. She completed her undergraduate degree when she was nineteen, married her husband Bob and they both proceeded with their graduate work at Emory University. Over the years, she has worked as a Chemist at Dupont in New Jersey, and as a Microbiologist and Toxicologist in various states such as; Georgia, Kentucky and Florida. In 1982 she and her husband bought and ran two retail stores for fifteen years in downtown Atlanta which he managed and she became buyer, treasurer, and store decorator for their toy store and cookie store. At this time, she also pursued a career as Manager of Research and Development in Toxicology at Ciba Vision (Novardis), a contact lens company.

Christie now lives in central Florida and after her husband died in 2000, she concentrated on writing her memoirs of her fifty years with him. They had two children, a boy and a girl. Christie has completed book one of twenty years and has given a copy to her children and grandchildren. She is now writing the second book for them since she has always felt that it would seem so heartbreaking to leave this life and have the ones she loves not know who she and her husband really were. She's been with the Writing Group since 2000. Her fellow writers agree that if she turned her amazing talents to fiction, her first book would be a sure best seller.

MOTHER

Memoir

by Christie Seiler

Mother began speaking in her soft, quiet voice while her children and grandchildren sat around her. As her memories filled her mind like a radiant dream spinning out across the years, it was as if we had discovered a dog-eared photograph album, the sepia snapshots, not faded at all, but clear and sharp-edged as ever. Mother was a born storyteller and when she spoke, we were transported back to 1910 as we envisioned her as a six year old standing on her tiptoes on the bathroom toilet seat, peering through the dirty window of the 'Home for the Friendless' orphanage.

Her hazel eyes swam in pools of tears and as the teardrops spilled over her long lashes, they created rivulets down her smudgy cheeks. She twirled her wispy blonde hair and wiped her running nose on her torn sleeve as she stuck her wrinkled thumb back in her mouth.

Watching the other children running to the barbed wire fence to grab a few candies from the visitors on the other side, she quietly chanted a litany over and over, "I want my mama."

That morning the matron had inspected each child's bed by pulling down the blankets and sniffing the sheets. When she reached Mable's bed she snatched her out of her mall, wet cocoon of warmth and in a loud, ominous voice told her she would sleep on the hard metal springs without a mattress until she stopped wetting the bed. She grabbed one of Mable's feet and hit the sole with a ruler, screaming at her that she would stay in the bathroom until she could remember what a toilet was for. Mable sat down on the cold floor and leaned against the large four-footed tub. As her face crumbled into tears once more, she tried to recall the last time she had been home with her mama. Images tumbled through her thoughts as she remembered how cold their cabin was and how her small feet and hands had ached as she sat hunched on a stool in front of the fireplace. The wind whistled in through the cracks between the logs of the cabin, making the ashes glow briefly. She was only four then and her six-year-old brother, Earl huddled close to her as her older sister Edith knelt beside them watching the embers die away.

"Edith, I'm cold," Mable whined plaintively.

Eight-year-old Edith quickly glanced at the dark figure in the corner who was singing softly to herself. "Hush, Mable, don't disturb mama, she's so sick. Marion will be home soon with some firewood."

It was very dark when they heard Marion enter the cabin with a bundle of wood. The small candle cast a shadow on the faces of his brothers and sisters wrapped in their ragged coats, as they gaze expectantly at him.

'What can a cripple like me do?' he wondered. *'Me and Bessie can't take the place of Ma and Pa.'*

Bessie stumbled in with her bundle of wood as she peered over Marion's misshapen shoulder.

"Oh! Edith, the fire is out! How will we ever get it started?"

At that moment she noticed her mama crouched on the floor, pulling imaginary bugs from her hair. "Marion, I think you should go fetch Aunt Nancy."

Nancy Rogers, the children's great aunt, was the local midwife and she often found that people who could not afford the price of a doctor would send for her in desperation.

As soon as Marion was able to start a small fire in the grate, he scrambled through the door as fast as his twisted body could move. He was so tired and hungry and felt so alone as he hurried down the road, his thoughts scattered by the wind. *'What is wrong with Ma and where did Pa go?'* He had heard Uncle Jim say that Pa had run off to California with a woman and had left Ma alone with her seven kids. *'Doesn't he know that I can't take care of Ma and my brothers and sisters without help?'* he wondered.

Today he had worked with one of their neighbors until the moon slid behind the dark clouds, picking the last of this season's cotton. Tomorrow, he would ask Edith to walk to the country store to get some cornmeal and beans with the money he had earned. Maybe the few pennies that ten-year-old Bessie had received for ironing clothes today would buy enough milk for baby Corinne and two year old Walter. *'How could he possibly feed six children and him?'*

He was puzzled at the change that had come over his Ma since Corinne was born and his Pa had left. He could remember when she had laughed and played with the younger kids, her dark curls and shiny smile reflected in the faces of everyone in the cabin, her brown eyes sparkling with fun. Now there was no more laughter and singing. "Maybe Aunt Nancy will know what to do," he sighed.

Later Marion breathed a sigh of relief as the steady crunch of the buggy wheels rolled through the deep grooves in the dirt road. He had been so relieved when he had arrived at Aunt Nancy's cabin just minutes before and had found her at home. When Marion explained why he was there, she quickly grabbed her bag and led him to her buggy. Marion leaned back in his seat, savoring this rare means of travel as he thought, *'Aunt Nancy will know what to do,'* realizing she had lifted a load from his small, twisted shoulders.

When they reached the cabin, it was immediately apparent that something was terribly wrong. His mother was sitting on the windowsill screaming as the children huddled in the corner.

"Marion, you and Bessie look after the children. I'm taking your mother with me," Nancy ordered.

That was the last time Mable remembered seeing her kind, gentle mother. The following morning, her aunt told them their mother was very sick and had gone away to recover. She gathered up the children's belongings and drew Mable, Edith, Bessie and Earl around her as she spoke softly to them, "Children, I need all of you to be very brave, for you will be going to live in an new place for awhile until your mother is well."

"How could Aunt Nancy have sent us to this place? Why did she let Marion and Walter and that cry baby, Corinne stay with her?" Mable whimpered plaintively as she sucked her thumb.

She picked up a small piece of soap and started drawing pictures on the old bathtub. At least her brother, Earl, lived in the dormitory next door and her big sisters Bessie and Edith slept in the beds next to her. They worked in the laundry all day, ironing clothes so she wasn't able to see them very often.

Mable leaned back against the bathroom wall when suddenly, the door flew open and the matron pulled her up by one arm and shook her vigorously, screaming, "Get that thumb out of your mouth and get dressed." She gave her a shove as she continued to shriek, "Gather your clothes together immediately; you'll be leaving right away."

Mable stumbled back to the large dormitory and to her cot. She dragged out an old wooden box from under her bed and quickly pulled on her red clay-dyed cornmeal sack dress. *What kind of punishment were they planning now?'* she thought. She wrapped her few remaining clothes in one of her large kerchiefs and sat down on the bed, tucking her bare feet beneath her.

At that moment, Edith and Bessie ran into the room dancing up and down. "We're going home with Aunt Nancy and Sis, they're waiting for us in the wagon," they exclaimed. Mable jumped off the bed, gave a little skip of happiness and then ran back to kiss her two sisters.

After their departure from the 'home', threatening storm clouds rolled across the sky as thunder gave way to a distant murmur and a gentle pattering of rain fell on the black buggy. As they rode along Ponce de Leon Avenue towards Decatur, Georgia, twelve-year-old Bessie looked longingly at each familiar building of the little town, gray and still in the afternoon light. In the ditches beside the road, wild, yellow daises bloomed in patches so large it looked as though pieces of sun had dropped to earth and shattered upon the grass as the flowers bent over from the weight of the jeweled water on their blossoms.

She could hardly wait to get to her aunt's cabin. When they finally arrived, its sagging roof and missing shingles made the place look tired around the edges. The yard was choked with weeds and scrawny chickens pecked at the dirt and complained loudly, yet to the children it was a safe haven. There were only four rooms in the small cabin where the two aunts and their sister Martha (the children's grandmother) and their mother lived.

Although none of the neighbors had much more than the Roger's family, they all pitched in to build a large kitchen with a dirt floor for them. In this small neighborhood they helped one another even though each one suffered and went hungry from time to time, as they struggled to survive in the rural south of 1910. The Civil war had been over for forty-five years, yet the intervening time had been hard, especially for the many unmarried or widowed women.

The days and weeks of summer ran into one another like a flowing river for the young children and each day was a new adventure. One morning as Mable grabbed the broom woven from corn shucks, dust moats danced in the column of sunlight slanting through the windows. She looked around as she quickly swept the dirt floor of the kitchen. It was such a nice floor; no one worried or screamed when water spilled on it like they did at the 'home'. When she finished her chores, she grabbed her bonnet and ran out of the house, as a covey of quail scurried across the road in front of her.

"Aunt Nancy," she called over her shoulder, "I'm going to the springs to help Bessie and Edith gather firewood for the wash tub."

As she approached the woods behind her house, she gazed up at the apple trees blooming in scented explosions of white as her footsteps lagged, enjoying the sun and the simple act of strolling through the lovely summer day. The blackberry bushes were already in bloom and the bees filled the air with a pleasant hum.

She picked up a seedcase from a maple tree nearby and flicked the boomerang shaped seed into the air and watched it whirl and dance in the light breeze before it floated slowly to the ground.

"Come on, Mable, help us carry this wood over to Ma and Sis," Bessie ordered as she approached her sisters.

Struggling, they pulled the heavy logs over to the springs near the washtub so the adults could build a large fire under it. As their mother threw the clothes into the hot water, the children stood around and stirred the clothes while the water boiled. The familiar scents of harsh soap that the aunts had made from lye and fat, the wet cotton and the burning wood wreathed around them. As Sis rinsed and wrung out the clothes, the children skipped back and forth, spreading them along the rows of blackberry bushes growing beside the springs. Wash days were so much fun in the summer for after the clothes were hung up to dry they always made a dam and went swimming in the creek formed by the springs.

Back at the cabin, Nancy stood for a moment in front of the old woodstove and stirred the rabbit stew she was making for supper. Steam slipped through the iron oven door carrying with it the mouth-watering aroma of biscuits baking. As she wiped her sweaty forehead with her arm, she took a large pinch of salt from the wooden box beside the stove. The pine lid thumped back into place as she sprinkled the coarse white granules into the stew. She ran her hands along her rumpled apron and sighing she walked over to the table and slumped on the hard bench, enjoying the quiet that stole over the house as she sat thinking about the baby she had delivered that morning. The birth had been long and agonizing and Nancy had almost lost both of them. *What will her future be,'* she thought, *'there are already so many children in that family. If there were only some way to prevent women from getting pregnant so often.'*

As she sat there, her thoughts turned to her own youth. Would her life have been different if Robert had not been killed in the Civil War? His absence was still like a raw wound that would never heal, even after all these years. She still loved him dearly and placed a lighted candle in the window every night in his memory.

She sat recalling the end of the war as if it were yesterday. After the Yankee soldiers left, and hoards of rebels returned home, a new and different reality began to take place. No longer did soldiers fight, people fought; they fought hunger, crop failure and corruption of the Federal overseers as well as each other. Georgians had faced their darkest days.

"Where had time gone?" she asked reflectively.

At seventy-five, Nancy was feeling her mortality and as she grew older the wheel of time seemed to spin faster and faster, robbing her of her days and leaving her with only a lifetime of whirling, flashing images. She had spent her life pushing forward, studying the world of herbal medicine, constantly reading and trying new methods of healing. If only she could have gone to medical school, how much more she could have learned. *'Just look at me and Martha and Sarah,'* she thought, *'as long as women don't have the right to vote, very little will change. At least there's a law now giving women control over property they own, but there's still no laws providing for divorces, alimony or child support.'* She had tried to get support from James when he left Mary with seven children, but she met with so much resistance from the courts that she had given up. Nevertheless she had been able to keep the children from starving on the streets or losing their limbs in factories, she realized.

Her days with them were like golden coins, cherished for the joys they brought her. Tiredly she pushed to her feet, grabbed two buckets and headed outside to the cistern. She didn't have time to sit down, since her family would be home from the springs soon.

A BOATING ADVENTURE

One Labor Day our family, along with some of our friends, was invited to go boating and picnicking with the Inkes off the coast of Daytona Beach in a borrowed 36' yacht. As we left the dock for a late afternoon trip, we felt our spirits buoyed by the sea, gossamer and airborne, carried effortlessly upward toward the sun as it beat down on us.

A breeze scooted across the gentle waves, cooling the air as we sailed up the inlet. Ahead a conical red buoy bobbed, listing lazily with the incoming tide as a pair of seagulls settled on it to survey the world with cold yellow eyes and to scream defiance at us.

As we sailed out the inlet, tidal currents surged through the channel and began to pitch the boat from bow to stern and the ever-present rush of the ocean to shore created background music and the cry of gulls became part of the orchestration. When we sailed up the coast the ship motored slowly along, weaving through the small sand dunes dense with foliage.

Verlan Inke, spotted a beautiful, secluded beach, "I think I'll anchor the boat out beyond the waves, but close to shore so we can swim over to the beach later if we want to," he announced as he pointed to the shore.

We spread our picnic supper of cold shrimp salad, potato salad and fruit on the table on the boat deck as the scent of the damp salt air drifted around us. The undisturbed water lay like cerulean silk, wrinkled only by a pair of pelicans out for a last evening swim. A cloud passed in front of the sun, its shadow trailed over us, bringing a momentary chill before it sailed on, leaving us in warmth.

After we finished eating, we carried our children over to the beach so that we could all take an evening swim before the sun set. As we leaped into the water, a trio of pelicans flew in military formation, climbing and rolling in unison, abruptly dropping with a dizzying headfirst dive into the sea, with a trio of splashes – then up again with fishes in their beaks.

While we swam out beyond the waves, the children waded in and out of the surf on a long walk down the beach as the waves lapped gently on the sand. From a distance we could hear their shrieks as they tried to catch the terns that fluttered overhead.

After our swim, we all sat on the rocks near the jetty as the wind came in soft gusts, laden with moisture, blowing soaking mist into our faces. A sea-gull flew overhead and we tipped our heads to watch its graceful passage, wings painted pink by the light of the setting sun. As we watched the sun drape itself along the water of the inlet to the west, the sky towards the east deepened into purple where already a star or two showed dimly on the crest.

As Lesli stared at the sparkling sand on the beach, she looked up, eyes alight and spoke with wonder in her voice, "Look, pieces of the sun have dropped to earth on the sand and have broken apart all over the beach."

I nodded as I looked into her eyes, "It looks like the beach has turned into a glittering fairyland doesn't it?"

Lesli beamed, realizing I had not dismissed her thought as ridiculous or unimportant. Bob looked at me and smiled, his gaze drawing mine as the beach draws the surf.

We decided to swim back to the boat and change clothes before it became too dark. Afterwards, we sat on deck and watched the darkness descend on the distant waves like a shawl fashioned of lilac mist draping itself over looming dark shoulders, bathing them in violet light, softening them. We fell silent, watching the moon drift among dark clouds that moved above the lilac-tinted water, pushed by the wind into a slow gliding dance. As we left this beautiful beach and headed toward the inlet, we realized the day had slipped by as easily as our boat had moved through the water, a lovely day of countless wonders with our friends and family.

As we approached the inlet, the lonely ringing of a bell buoy drifted up from the hidden sandbars of the shoals. Caught in a fantasy woven of moonlight, Verlan studied the shore and noticed far to the south, the jagged line of trees and tidal marshes. The far horizon was lost in the darkness, but the heaving, restless ocean went on forever. Far out, the lighthouse flashed its warning – one short beam and two long beams.

After we entered the inlet, the water was black and still, except where the moonlight reached across in a wide path, and the trees scattered along its edge were tipped with silver leaves. The water stirred, scattering the light into glittering fragments that shone for a moment, then faded into the blackness. Far in the distance, the red and green riding lights of fishing boats dipped in the swell and sent shimmering reflections down into the inky water.

Suddenly overhead the clouds grew dark and threatening and the wind rose, stirring the water into white-capped silver waves. The leaden sky seemed to sink lower and lower, until the clouds, heavy with moisture, rested on the choppy surface of the water. At that moment, Verlan seemed to lose control of the boat and it hit a sandbar, sending all of us forward with a sudden abrupt motion.

"Lesli, Keith," I shouted my children's names into the wind as my voice was pulled from my mouth.

Verlan immediately assessed the situation, "Sorry folks, I'm afraid we've run aground." After attempting to rock the boat back and forth with the engine, he announced, "I guess all of the adults will have to jump over board and try to push the boat off the bar."

At that moment the tension was as thick as the shroud of clouds that surrounded us as we turned and stared at each other.

When I swung my legs over the side, I looked at Bob whose hands were tensed as he gripped the rail, and I remembered in every detail his square hands, scared by calluses, his blunt fingers that had touched me with such sensitivity. Bob was steady and practical and as I leaned close to him, I touched his arm to reassure myself.

He instantly covered my hand with his, as he seemed to feel my distress. "It will be all right," he assured me.

The defined bones of his face made him look as purposeful and intense as I knew him to be as he swung his legs over and fell into the water. During our climb overboard, we noticed the sky was lowered to a menacing greenish-black. We struggled through the wild, broken water of the inlet where hidden currents tugged and sucked at our feet, the wind tore at our hair and whipped it about like seaweed and plankton flashed phosphorescent in the water around us.

While the five of us pushed and tugged at the boat, I kept thinking of sharks and eels and of my children being left orphans. Finally our struggles paid off and the boat slowly floated away from the grip of the bar.

When we climbed on board, the children cheered and as Keith ran over to us, he spoke in a loud voice, "Even though you were afraid, you were able to go to the bathroom while you were in the water, right, mom?"

We felt a flash of wry humor. We take pride in our intelligent children, and then we have to live with the fact that they see through us.

I turned the conversation toward them and away from images that burned in my lungs like cold winter air, hoping the memory of this night would be smeared with a chalky eraser.

After we reached the dock, we quickly loaded the car and headed for home, happy to be safe on shore at last. With the hush of the night slipping quickly toward dawn and the children asleep around me, I curled up in the silence of the car. Time ceased to tick; the world had slipped into a silent dimension in which we were the only four people on earth. How fortunate I was to have my family safe and have Bob for a husband. No other wife in the world could possibly be as treasured as I am.

Biography of
Joan Heavey

Joan Heavey's story *ROAD TO THE GALLOWS* is the first chapter of her novel-in-progress *Fortune Maker*, a legend narrating what happened to the notorious pirate Captain William Kidd's fortune in jewels and ancient gold coins. The story's introduction is a tantalizing quotation by Honore de Balzac, the famed 1800's French writer and philosopher: "Behind every great fortune is a great crime."

Joan often creates novels under the pen name, Joan Randolph, and has enjoyed the writing business for many years. She began her career as a copywriter for an NBC radio affiliate in Baton Rouge, Louisiana. Later, she worked as a newspaper writer and editor. In the 80's she published the first newspaper for women, The Maryland Woman's Journal, then moved to the Eastern Shore of Maryland with her husband John, where they enjoyed playing golf and bridge with friends at the Prospect Bay Country Club. While living in Grasonville, Maryland, Joan became first president of the Eastern Shore Writer's Association. She was born in Gardiner, Maine, educated at the University of Maine at Farmington and now lives and writes at The Villages, Florida.

ROAD TO THE GALLOWS

historical fiction

by Joan Heavey

May 23, 1701

Time hangs heavily on a desperate man who has suffered stunning misfortune. Misery dominates his thoughts, blocking attempts to sleep. In the case of the wretched prisoner rotting away in the gloomy bowels of Newgate Prison in London, forces beyond his wildest imaginings had been at work conspiring against him. He was a dead man before his case ever reached the Old Bailey.

Unaware of his fate in the beginning, the formerly wealthy New Yorker Captain William Kidd had expected no more than a slap on the wrist when Crown authorities heard his story, then freedom. Month after month, he'd waited for powerful associates to come forward with the truth about his last voyage. Only belatedly, and to his horror, did Kidd begin to comprehend that his co-conspirators wanted him dead. They would not help. Every day he lived was a threat to their reputations, to their lives. Yes, he had lost their money – and *his*. The fateful voyage had been a disaster.

Crown officials had caught up with him at sword point in Boston, later charging him with piracy and several false crimes, the most outrageous being the murder of his head gunner on the *Adventure Galley*, William Moore.

Kidd had been thrown into Boston's notorious Stone Prison with no proper clothing to see him through the frigid winter of 1700. In his icy cell, alone and despondent, he had nearly died from exposure. Only when his keepers realized that Kidd was close to death, did they provide enough clothing and cover for his survival. Crown authorities wanted him alive, so they could ship him to London for a very public trial. Kings orders.

Kings orders! Kidd had fumed. What in God's name was going on here? How could they send him to London? King William was one of his partners.

They did.

On this notable morning, May 23, 1701, Captain Kidd sat on his louse-infected mat at Newgate prison staring blankly into space. A broken man, weary from no sleep in weeks, he gulped another swallow of rum from a rusty tin cup, barely aware of the three prison acquaintances who for hours had tried to make light conversation. Kidd had adsorbed little of the chatter, but now, even in his alcohol soaked brain, he knew he must face the business of the day, a parade to his death as thousands watched in macabre fascination.

"Captain," a handsome young and dirty-faced pick-pocket named Scab, spoke in a gentle manner. "Axin' yer pardon, sir, but it's nigh time to be getting dressed. Mulrooney 'as just delivered yer new shirt, fresh laces and some soap." Scab placed the items beside Kidd's fresh uniform, pausing to admire the quality. "Aye, you'll be making a fine appearance in those, lest you canna' walk from too much rum." He chuckled momentarily at the thought of the dignified Kidd who'd become a much-publicized celebrity, stumbling, or falling down, at an awkward moment on the road to his death. Scab caught the menacing eye of his inmate friend Jake Carot, who was helping Kidd to a standing position.

"You'll be pleased, sir, with the effort Mulrooney has done for you. He even wrote a ballad in your honor," said Carot, glaring unhappily at Scab.

The delivery boy the men referred to was well known to all Newgate prisoners and guards. Sean Mulrooney, an ambitious little Cockney ran a coffee shop opposite the prison, and astonishingly, had the run of the place. Everybody knew Mulrooney whose primary business was supplying the prison dwellers with food, spirits and special services –

for a price of course. He also carried messages, wrote letters for the illiterate and composed ballads for sale about notorious Newgate prisoners.

Captain Kidd was of special interest to Mulroony. Unknown to himself, Kidd had a large and sympathetic following. Many citizens insisted that he'd been unfairly accused and tried. They knew Crown authorities had prevented Kidd from seeking legal help – help that could have saved his life. The gentlemanly captain had been illegally kept for months in solitary confinement and certain trial witnesses had lied under threat of their lives. Yet, Kidd's harsh sentence came as a shock in this day and time. Piracy was a common experience by all men of the sea. The sentence had created intense sympathy from his public admirers.

Not only was the enterprising Mulrooney personally fond of Kidd, but his arrest and harsh treatment had become fodder for Mulrooney's eager pockets. He'd already worked for weeks making posters to sell on the day of the hanging. His biggest creative prize that would sell for months to come were two emotional ballads he'd composed. They'd bring in big money today at Wapping and Execution Dock.

As soon as Mulrooney made this last delivery to Kidd – the soap, the laces and the formal shirt, he took his pay. The two men shook hands with affection.

In his numbed condition the captain pondered his last desperate moments of struggle, following a miserable two years of jail, Kidd welcomed the end to his misery. The fortune in treasure he had hidden in a far-away cave no longer mattered.

In the last few hours before his capture in Boston, Kidd had tried to describe the hiding place to his wife. He explained how Sarah could hire a ship, captained by a friend, for the short sail from Boston to a remote island in Maine. But Sarah had angrily refused. She was terrified that she too would be thrown in prison.

She'd enjoyed the years of marriage to the prominent captain. That William Kidd, an elegant and proud gentleman, esteemed citizen of New York, retired businessman, trading captain-merchant, member of the Trinity Church and attentive lover, had stolen her heart the first day they'd met.

It happened during the spring of 1691. Young Sarah was married to a New York Dutchman, William Oort, when Kidd appeared at her door to inquire about the sale of her home.

For years, Kidd had admired a distinguished mansion on the Hudson River, visible by all ships that sailed into New York Harbor. The property at 121 Pearl Street sat facing a sod dike that held back the river. The yellow house stood three stories tall, featuring graceful architectural placement of windows and entrance with an inviting pair of circular walk-up stairs to the front door.

When the forty-year old bachelor heard mention that the handsome house was for sale, Kidd could barely contain his excitement sparing no time to reach the owner, the beautiful and wealthy Sarah Oort, who had inherited the property from her first husband, Alderman William Cox.

At the time, Sarah and her servants were tending her fatally-ill second husband whose decline had been long, painful and expensive. Sarah had decided to sell the waterfront property and move further up the river to her Saw Kill farm which earned a considerable profit from garden crops and an apple orchard. Maintaining two households and staffs had become a financial strain. In spite of her love of the New York social scene, Sarah put the house up for sale. William Kidd became her best prospect in more ways than one.

Kidd and Sarah met many times that memorable spring, excitedly chatting away in the downstairs parlor, disquieting as it may have been to hear the piteous moans and scrambling servants attending the tragedy upstairs.

Captain Kidd couldn't keep his eyes off the enchanting young woman – nor his hands and lips. Their fascination for each other grew daily. In time the household chaos quieted, as Oort sank into a fretful coma – then death. Kidd took out a marriage license two weeks later.

He remained awestruck at Sarah's beauty, grace and musical accomplishment. Yet, Kidd was dismayed to discover that this lively, intelligent woman could neither read or write, other than her signature, a common situation in the 1700's.

Negotiations concerning the sale of the dwelling ended when Kidd purchased the impressive property from Sarah, and married her shortly thereafter. They lived in the New York home for five happy years – *until his fateful mission.*

Damn! Damn! He'd known all along that the proposed voyage would be his undoing. Kidd's old friend from sailing days in the West Indies, Captain Hewson, had advised against the trip.

"A fool's mission, my fine friend," Hewson had warned. "At sea, so many years, your luck has been extraordinary. How many times have you faced sure death or financial ruin? Indeed, all of us are guilty of a little pirating, here and there, but times are changing. God knows, you don't need the money. Why would you consider such a mission?"

"Aye, that's my thinking, as well." Kidd nodded in agreement. "I've had my share of luck and good fortune. I'll send word to Livingston and Governor Bellomont to find themselves another captain."

Robert Livingston, friend and financial partner of Lord Bellomont, recently appointed Governor of New York, refused to be put off. Kidd was their man, they insisted, no other would do.

Kidd had met Livingston in London in 1698. Both New Yorkers, each was in London on business. Livingston, a strange-looking fellow, tried to appear normal in spite of a rigidly frozen jaw and a misshapen nose. Yet Kidd was attracted to the man who was talented in financing. He was also brainy and seemed to know everybody important in London, including King William.

Now they wanted Kidd to sail for them on a mission that not only was foolhardy, but dangerous. For months, Kidd refused with gentlemanly excuses, but they pressured him with no let up, wondering out loud how any captain who swore loyalty to the Crown, could ignore so clear a call to serve King William. They darkly suggested that Kidd's refusal to accept this commission would question his loyalty. Kidd might even have trouble getting his ship free of customs for his return to New York.

Upset, he finally agreed. "Aye, I'll do it. But the cost will be great. Where does the money come from?"

Livingston had smiled mysteriously, as if raising 100,000 pounds would be no problem. Bellomont and others put up four-fifths and Kidd and Livingston the rest in good-performance bonds. For Kidd's part, he was forced to sell a ship he owned waiting to be loaded in

Plymouth. He had to borrow further funds from English financial sources with whom he'd done previous business. In all, he managed to raise twenty thousand pounds.

That's how the voyage to the Indian Ocean came about. Kidd himself a gentleman pirate who had never been charged with illegal behavior, (of which there had been ample) if one took into account easily ignored laws and petty rules, in particular those dealing with the Americas. His mission: a pirate sent out to catch and arrest other pirates, most of whom Kidd knew and had dealt with for years. Loot seized from those outlaw vessels would be used to pay Kidd, his crew, as well as his backers, plus ten percent to King William. As things turned out, the monarch never did pay the money he'd promised, but his name appeared on a written document, critically important to Kidd. A commission from the King was considered invaluable.

Still, the voyage was a chancy proposition. Every pirate whom Kidd knew would fight to the death to protect his stolen riches, thus assuring fierce battles against pirates who loved to fight, a grave danger to Kidd who'd lost his fighting spirit.

Even if he successfully attacked two, or three, known cutthroats and seized all their treasure, his personal reward would be slight.

Yet Kidd had no option other than to put the best face on a troublesome proposition. Once he got to sea, he was the boss – all power was his and he understood its use, so he accepted the commission.

In spite of good intentions, everything that could have gone wrong, did indeed go wrong. At the beginning, with money given him for the mission, Kidd purchased a ship in England and spent the better part of three months having it outfitted and armed. Installed were thirty-four cannons, and ports for twenty-three sweeps on each side to enable rowing in calm weather. The ship weighed 267 tons and took a crew of seventy men.

Kidd named her the *Adventure Galley*.

The first foreshadowing that this voyage was headed for problems happened as Kidd sailed the *Adventure Galley* from England. Members of his crew insulted sailors as they passed a Royal frigate. The ship's captain angrily called Kidd on the carpet for questioning. As punishment, the admiral took fifty of Kidd's best sailors. In a fury, Kidd presented his papers to the royal commission. The admiral took note and sent fifty replacements back to the *Adventure Galley*. Alas, not the same experienced men that had been carefully trained.

The *Adventure Galley* was forced to sail with this trouble – making, bottom-of-the-barrel crew. Drunks and loners, many of whom had never been to sea.

His backers, annoyed that Kidd's preparations had required so much time, demanded that he get underway. To their great shock and annoyance, rather that heading south for the Indian Ocean and action, he sailed west for New York, explaining to his furious partners that he needed more time to train his sullen crew (of uncertain talents) and bring the ship up to fighting strength. The truth lay closer to his desire to see pretty Sarah and their daughter, Elizabeth.

In New York Sarah welcomed Kidd with open arms, delighted to hear that his work with the crew and ship might take another three months. They laughed and hugged each other.

"Ah, William, my love. I'm so happy to see you! The summer season is just beginning. We can go to the best affairs and I shall plan a grand ball in your honor. Perhaps even a 'bon voyage' party aboard the beautiful *Adventure Galley* just before you sail."

It was a wonderful summer. They went everywhere together. On cool mornings, Kidd would row Sarah and Elizabeth up the Hudson River for a picnic at her Saw Kill Farm. He was delighted to learn that another child was on the way, perhaps this time, a son?

The most impressive affair they attended was their own, the 'bon voyage' party Sarah had suggested. The event took place two days before the *Adventure Galley* sailed.

Sarah's servants had busied themselves for days shopping and cooking, selecting the finest wines from Kidd's wine cellar. The day before the party, Sarah sent aboard a rare Oriental rug, adding a luxurious touch to the *Adventure Galley's* deck. Kidd's finest Madeira further enhanced the impressiveness of the occasion.

Personal invitations had been hand delivered to prominent citizens. Everybody came: New York Governor (and Kidd's partner) Lord Bellomont and his young frivolous wife; Attorney General, James Graham; others attending included James Emmot and John Gardiner, both good friends of Kidd's, plus a personal friend of many years, Duncan Campbell, the well-known Boston bookseller.

Sarah's brother, the handsome Samuel Bradley, a prominent and successful New York businessman, also attended the party. Bradley had signed on as a crew member, excited at the chance for a grand adventure. Kidd had reluctantly agreed to the inclusion of Bradley after warning both Sarah and Bradley of the dangers and life-threatening situations common to all men of the sea. Unknowing innocents, they laughed away Kidd's concerns, yet Sarah would never again see her beloved brother.

The party went wonderfully. Sarah, in her most impressive silk frock, not yet showing her pregnancy, brought Elizabeth aboard early. Kidd introduced his wife and daughter to his crew, all dressed for the occasion in their 'Sunday best', colorfully disguising the reality that most of them were pirates and cutthroats, eager to get to sea and fighting – be damned with fancy parties and important persons. Yet Kidd was amused to observe his men actually enjoying the occasion, several of them behaving with gallantry, bowing to the pretty ladies, answering questions with pride, sometimes with startling intelligence.

The *Adventure Galley* left New York September 6, 1696, and headed south for the eight-thousand mile run to the Indian Ocean where a large amount of pirate activity took place. Kidd went to great lengths to keep his written mission secret, no point in warning his pirate acquaintances that he'd been sent to arrest them. Yet, somehow word slipped out.

In early December, Kidd fell in with a group of English warships. They were, as usual, short-handed, their commander envious of Kidd's royal commissions and his now well trained crew. It came as no surprise when Kidd, his first officer and Samual Bradley, Sarah's brother, were invited to join the admiral and some of his officers for wine and dinner aboard the admiral's ship. Kidd recalling his recent bad luck with the royal frigate as he left England, reluctantly accepted the invitation and had a crew member row him and his two associates to the nearby warship.

The evening was filled with friendliness and conviviality. The wine impressive. Finally, the subject came around to the warship's need for extra crew. Kidd sympathized, but this time he was prepared when the request came forth.

"Captain Kidd, sir. I'd appreciate it a great kindness if you were to offer me twenty of your men," said the commander.

Kidd smiled, appearing cooperative. "I completely understand the situation. It shouldn't be a problem."

When Kidd and his party returned to the *Adventure Galley* late in the evening, he ordered his crew to set sail and was far beyond the horizon by the time the royal commander realized he'd been tricked. No legal complaint here, Kidd had recorded: it was a request, not an order!

Now beyond the Cape, Kidd entered fighting waters, but showed little indication for action. He faced two choices: go east toward numerous pirate ships and their captains, most of whom he knew by name, or head west to the less threatening Mozambique Channel. He sailed west, hoping to avoid four men whose captures were listed in his commission from the king and recorded in papers written by Livingston and Lord Bellomont. Longtime acquaintances of Kidd, the pirates' names were Thomas Tew, John Ireland, Captain Thomas Wake and Captain William Maze. Kidd hoped to avoid all four, but if he happened to come upon one, or two, he felt prepared to perform his duty.

In the Bay of Tulear, off the coast of Madagascar, Kidd and his crew met with an appalling disaster. The critically ill owner of a Barbados sloop staggered aboard the *Adventure Galley*, begging for medical assistance. Kidd, horrified lest his crew become contaminated, ordered the man off his ship, but the unfortunate ship-owner dropped dead. Kidd quickly set sail, but the infected ship shadowed the *Adventure* all the distance up the straights where Kidd planned to careen his ship for cleaning and repair.

The plague hit Kidd's crew within ten days. By weeks end, fifty of his hundred men died horrible, messy deaths, attended by the *Adventure's* ship surgeon, Dr. Robert Bradenham.

His voyage goals destroyed, his crew weak and furious, Kidd felt certain that he would be attacked by the shadowing ship. It failed to happen, perhaps because the watchful sloops crew decided the *Adventure* was too well-armed with too many sailors surviving the plague. No attack took place. On a near-deserted Arabian beach, Kidd replaced his dead crew members with 30 ragged, inexperienced vagabonds – men he could barely trust and who spoke no English. All this, facing failure, trying to deal with surviving crew members, several of whom were still ill, including Sarah's brother Samuel Bradley.

Finally, the dam gave way, Kidd could no longer bear the pressure from his unruly sailors. On July 25, 1697, much in the fashion of the pirates he had been commissioned to hunt down, Kidd ordered his men ready for an attack after learning that fifteen ships were in a nearby port, many laden with valuable cargo and rich, be-jeweled Moslems bound to and from Mecca.

"Come on boys!" Kidd shouted, "We'll make money out of that fleet!" In no time, his suddenly enthusiastic crew loaded shot, cleaned, greased and oiled the cannon, filled powder baskets, spread water, sand and blankets on the decks to kill expected fires. Directed by the ship's doctor, they arranged space for wounded shipmates. Lastly, they passed out small arms, then waited.

On alert, they watched outside the channel for eleven days. Finally on August 15, their patience paid off. Up went the red pirate's pennant, demanding immediate surrender of an approaching vessel, or battle to death.

Kidd's expert and experienced eyes zeroed in on the cumbersome merchantman and headed the *Adventure* in to intercept. To his shock, dismay and fury, his chosen prey ship was escorted by three well-armed guard vessels, headed by an East Indian Company ship, the *Spectre*. Kidd gamely fired a broadside, but the *Spectre* hoisted English colors.

So far, he'd met with nothing but failure and extraordinary bad luck. Word would travel like a lightning strike to the Admiralty in London that the *Adventure Galley* had turned pirate. At this very moment, Kidd knew officers of the East India Company were busily recording his attempted attack.

Kidd pondered his fate in acute depression: he was without money; he'd turned pirate, yet had nothing to show for it, and no way to pay his crew.

And now, a personal tragedy faced him. Sarah's brother, Samual Bradley, whose health had never been robust, had become ill at the same time the crew had been exposed to the plague. With special food and care from Kidd and Dr. Bradenham, Bradley appeared to survive the first ravages. The youthful Bradley was ill again – seriously ill – and begged his brother-in-law to send him ashore.

From years of experience, Kidd had an instinct concerning such matters: he knew Bradley would die and tried to convince him to remain onboard and take his chances, but Bradley insisted. Kidd sent the fatally-ill man ashore, trying not to envision the scene when he faced Sarah with the tragic news of her brother's death.

Adding to Kidd's agony, his crew loomed on the edge of mutiny, furious that the captain refused to attack his own countrymen. On deck one day, his chief gunner William Moore, weakened from his bout of cholera and feeling terrible, angrily accused Kidd of being a coward – afraid to attack and plunder. They remained unaware of the *Adventure Galley's* true mission.

Kidd rebuked Moore for his insolence, but Moore refused to back off. Finally the captain reached his boiling point. Kidd grabbed a wooden bucket and cracked Moore on the side of his head. Unconscious, the gunner's mates carried him below deck to the surgeon, who was drinking heavily. The following morning Moore was dead, the crew in a greater fury.

After Moore's death, Kidd had to face the seriousness of his failures. He'd been at sea for fourteen months with nothing to show for his good intentions and unanticipated bad luck. He was six months overdue on his agreement with Lord Bellomont (to meet in Boston and surrender pirate ships he'd captured, their cargos and treasures as well). So far, he'd met with nothing but failure and bad luck.

In despair and smarting from failure, Captain Kidd returned to America and was arrested. Crown officials, in their frenzy to grab all riches and property in Kidd's name, had even absconded with twenty-five crowns belonging to Sarah's maid. They took everything of Kidd's: the Pearl Street house, his bank accounts and his part-ownership in a trading vessel. They knew Kidd had valuable treasure hidden in some remote place. They never came close to finding it. But they found him!

Until now, piracy against other countries, especially enemies like Spain and France, had been generally ignored. Much thievery and looting had historically been financed and encouraged by English monarchs, such as Elizabeth I, who hired notorious captains and cutthroats calling them 'adventurers' or 'explorers.' Thieves and plunderers had long been shrouded in respectability, their crimes hard to prove. Later hundreds of sailing men went into business for themselves, keeping all their loot. Suddenly piracy increased worldwide, but now there were terrible consequences. Piracy must be stopped, especially because England earned no profits from it. Captain Kidd's capture and death set up by the monarchy would become a warning to all men of the sea.

The Gallows

As has been true for centuries, dying in the 1700's was an event attended by one's friends and relatives. In the case of public execution, family and friends hovered at the scene, as well as thousands of on-lookers anxious to witness the excitement of the day. Painfully for the condemned, often enemies were there to witness one's final humiliation, perhaps to grin or gloat.

In Captain Kidd's case, those attending were a collection of Crown authorities and prison employees, many citizens who had sat through his trial, and members of the Old East India Company, led by Coji Baba, the Indian executive who had brought suit against Kidd for attacking their ships. With all the celebrity hangings, a crowd of thousands in a holiday mood, stepped lively escorting the condemned along the road to execution dock.

Relatives were especially welcomed by those condemned to die at the gallows. Customarily, the hangman would assist the trembling and blind-folded victim up a wobbly ladder. Then at a signal, push him off the scaffold. Because the drop was only a few feet, many victims survived long minutes of agony, gagging and jerking about in desperate struggle, dying of strangulation rather than a broken neck. In such cases, a victims friends and associates were permitted to rush forward, jump up and grab the twitching body, pulling down to break his neck and end the misery.

Captain Kidd's execution was set for May 23, 1701. The clerk at Old Baily had read in a subdued voice –

"You have been tried by the laws of the land. Nothing remains but that the sentence be passed according to the law. And the sentence is this: You shall be taken from the place whence you came, to the place of execution and there be severally hanged by your neck until you be dead. And may the Lord have mercy on your soul."

"My Lord," said the stunned Kidd. "That is a very hard sentence. For my part, I am the most innocent person. I have been sworn against by perjured persons."

Captain Kidd and several other condemned pirates were returned to Newgate to await their execution slated to take place at Wapping, a squalid marshland neighborhood whose inhabitants were, for the most part, London's poorest and disenfranchised seamen.

Newgate Prison: Cold. Damp. A place of hell. A stone horror of tiny cells and dark corridors that never saw daylight. Five stories that stank of mold, urine and feces. Neighborhood persons crossed the street in front of the prison, to avoid the smell that surrounded the ancient building. Many London physicians refused to enter its crowded squalor, ignoring serious illnesses caused by the filth.

Kidd was illegally kept in solitary confinement – strangely in the company of his young Malagasy slave who had arrived at Newgate chained to his master. During their year's confinement, Kidd *unsuccessfully* tried to teach the man English. In the end, the youth was bequeathed to Kidd's Newgate keeper.

On this day an enormous crowd gathered early at Execution dock and its many neighborhoods. By three o'clock the crowd swelled to three thousand irreverent onlookers as William Kidd, the gentleman pirate, blindfolded, his heart racing mercilessly, would be jerked away from the moldy scaffold, his body to be left in plain view for years for all who sailed.

The execution procession was scheduled to leave Newgate on the warm May afternoon at two o'clock. Marshall Cheeke of the Admiralty had hired three carts to haul ten prisoners, including Kidd, from Newgate prison to Execution Dock at Wapping. He had also contracted for temporary gallows that would hold a dozen men. The executioner would be paid one pound for each prisoner killed, plus the traditional shilling-sixpence for each noose.

Cheeke on horseback, resplendent in a colorful uniform lead the procession holding the silver oar of the Admiralty. His attire elegant when compared to the sheriffs and their assistants who rode as guards for the prisoners and crowd control. Their clothing was shabby, often unclean. It was their job to surround the wagon-like cart of the condemned.

The crowd in a jovial mood, jostled to come close to Captain Kidd, best-known of the accused criminals. They fought to touch him, to wish him well, some told him that he'd been unfairly treated by the Admiralty and the Crown.

Kidd was drunk, some suggested the 'life of the party.' This is surely an exaggeration, although there was no chance he might become sober, being constantly offered spirits from those close by. The carts carrying the condemned men halted three times as onlookers eagerly gave drink to keep the men's horror at a minimum.

Many in the crowd teased good naturedly, "Ay Captain, where'd you hide the treasure?" Loud laughter followed.

One onlooker near the captain's cart gave Kidd an astonishing piece of news – although two months old – but just received in London. He learned that Lord Bellomont, his persistent accuser, had died in New York. Kidd responded with a smile and requested that the cart stop, as individuals rushed forward to administer more rum, a tiny personal celebration over the New York governor's death.

At the end of the three mile journey, Kidd and his fellow pirates finally faced the roughhewn gallows. It was hastily and simply constructed: one wooden crossbeam, held up by two vertical upright beams, with a raised platform sturdy enough to hold the ten doomed prisoners, the executioner and two ministers.

At that moment, a dramatic scene took place, Marshall Cheeke, with an official appearing document in his hand, walked toward the condemned group. He pulled aside six men who had been granted last-minute pardons. Kidd and the crowd watched as tears began to run down the strained faces of the six men who had received the reprieves. They cried aloud, then trembling, dropped to their knees in prayer, astonished to be free. Two of the men were Kidd's loyal seamen. Four had served with Captain Culliford, a former competitor and enemy of Kidd.

The remaining four men would be hanged: Captain William Kidd, Darby Mullins an Irishman, who had sailed with Kidd. Mullins had recently survived a severe case of bloody flux and was in wretched health. The last men, Jean Duboise and Pierre Mingeneau were Frenchmen, now praying in their native tongue.

Each man was allowed his final say. The crowd was miraculously hushed: dying words ranked high in the day's entertainment. As it happened, the three sailors, dressed in ragged Newgate clothing, had little to say. But Kidd, resplendent in his colorful waistcoat and breeches, shouted out in drunken, slurred words that he had done nothing wrong. He was a helpless victim. He singled out Lord Bellomont and Robert Livingston, his former partners, as villains and liars.

Paul Lorraine, the Newgate Chaplin, whispered to Kidd that the time for anger was passed – that the captain should announce that God had rightly brought him to the gallows. Lorraine had a reputation for writing articles describing confessions made to him by condemned prisoners, which he sold for huge profit. Kidd ignored the preacher, but did offer, still in a drunken demeanor, confidence in God's mercy.

At that moment, the hangman and his assistants jerked the blocks away from under the platform. The four men only dropped six inches, insuring that their struggle would be long and terrifying.

But Captain Kidd didn't die. His rope broke and he fell to the ground. Dumbfounded to be breathing, although he'd experienced a powerful prelude of how it feels to expire by strangulation. He studied the three men dying above him as they jerked their legs and bodies in a macabre death dance. Within minutes their faces turned purple, urine seeped through their crotches and they died. The crowd roared, shocked that Kidd lived an additional fifteen minutes, having to observe a preview of how he would endure his final moments.

Kidd's unexpected fall had sobered him in a cruel manner. Standing patiently as the embarrassed hangman scrambled for new rope and a noose. An assistant hangman was sent to find another ladder. Now, Kidd announced that he was dying in Christian love with kind feelings for his fellow man. "My greatest regret," he called out in a clear voice, "is the thought of my beloved wife's sorrow over my shameful death."

The rattled hangman a second time kicked away the ladder. Captain Kidd met his death with little struggle.

Biography of
Allen Weintraub

Allan Weintraub is an enthusiastic member of the Village Writers. He attends nearly every meeting. Most weeks, he has something interesting and/or humorous to read to the group. He started writing only recently, but has a lifetime of adventures to write about, having lived in Florida, Louisiana, California, Rhode Island, Texas and Japan. He was born and raised in Boston, Mass.

During World War II, Alan flew as a Navy Pilot. He has also worked as a warehouse manager, in Florida real estate, and as a teacher and house husband. A sometime artist, he won the 'Best in Show" honors at an art show in Key West.

Allan Weintraub has nearly finished a mystery novel entitled *Con Man*, a story of a clever petty criminal who gets involved in a big jewel robbery and ends up in a government witness protection program 'safe house' where his past life begins to threaten his new one and a new love.

THE FREE BALLOON RIDE

Memoir

by Alan Weintraub

I received orders to the Naval Air Station at Lakehurst, New Jersey for flight training in Lighter-than-air-craft, otherwise known as airships. There were other names for them such as poopy bags, or gas bags, or balloons. Regardless of what you call them they are a flight vehicle unlike any I had flown before.

The airship is a large gasbag filled with helium, a nonflammable gas that provides the ship with sixty-four pounds of lift for every one thousand cubic feet of helium. In order to lift the material and personnel that make up the airship and its crew, it must be made to a great mass. Most modern airships are in the range of one-half million cubic feet. The bag is made of a cotton neoprene. Inside the bag, attached to the top, are catenary curtains from which cables are hung down. These cables are attached to the gondola, which hangs from the underside of the bag. The gondola is the platform that houses the personnel that operate the ship. Two small reciprocating engines are attached to the gondola, one on each side. Should these engines fail for some reason, the airship becomes a free balloon. It is for this reason that part of the lighter-than-air training involves a free balloon ride.

It was a cold winter day in January at Lakehurst, New Jersey. The weatherman had forecast frost but very little wind. A perfect day for a free balloon training flight. We were dressed in fur-lined jackets and pants held up by wide suspenders. On our feet were fur-lined boots and we had fur-lined gloves for our hands. We were a group of five newly commissioned Ensigns in the Navy. The instructor was a young Lieutenant. The hangars at Lakehurst were made for airships. They were big enough to house the German Zeppelin Hindenberg. For our small group of five trainees and one instructor, we felt lost in this huge structure built to house giants. A stake truck was driven into the hangar. On its rear was a folded-up free balloon, bundled like a large gift waiting to be unwrapped.

In unison we all pitched in to pull the ropes, and cloth, and basket from the back of the truck. Since it was so cold outside, the instructor decided to inflate the balloon inside the hangar. Helium bottles were positioned and attached to nozzles, and the balloon was slowly inflated as we all worked together spreading the lines that hung over the balloon and attached to the basket.

It was a sight to see, that huge balloon growing up right before our eyes. Final preparedness involved hanging forty pound sand bags around the outside of the basket and stowing the necessary equipment of compass, altimeter, maps, and a megaphone. Enough gas had been put into the balloon to make it quite light. So much so that we had to hold it down or it would take off without us. We all climbed into the basket, the five students and one instructor.

Since we were still in the hangar, a group of enlisted men literally carried us out to the mat away from the hangar. While this was being done, the instructor assigned each student a position in the basket. There was the sand man. He was to release sand from a tray, which had been filled from one of the forty pound sand bags. This would make us lighter and we would rise. There was the helium man. He would pull on the valve cord attached to a valve on the top of the balloon, which would release helium. This would make us heavy and we would go down. There was the compass man. He would yell out the direction we were floating over the landscape. And there was the altimeter man. He was to let us know our altitude. And finally there was the megaphone man. That would be the instructor. He would holler down to the stake truck, which would follow our flight on the ground to retrieve the balloon once we made our final landing. We were ready to take off.

Once we obtained a position in the morning air, we felt a slight breeze of about five knots. "Perfect," said the instructor, "Throw over a handful of sand."

The sandman responded with an, "Aye, aye Sir," and threw over a handful of sand.

The amount was so minute that nothing happened. Again the instructor ordered, "Throw over another hand full of sand."

Again the sandman responded. Nothing. The instructor was expecting the balloon to start up or at least move gently across the mat, but nothing. We were planted in one spot. Again the instructor ordered for more sand, and after a number of attempts we finally started bouncing across the mat. The gentle breeze was taking us from our starting point, not being light enough to fly, but just light enough to bounce us across the mat. The mat was a round area over a mile in diameter. As we bounced, throwing sand as we went, the pine trees at the end of the mat were growing in stature. As we closed in on the trees the instructor's voice pitch got higher and higher. Finally, with an imminent collision with the trees about to take place, the instructor hollered at the top of his lungs, "For God's sake, throw over a bag of sand."

Well, needless to say, the instructor's anxious conduct was responded to by all of us and in unison we all grabbed sand bags that were hanging over the side of the basket and threw them over on the ground. Losing a combined two hundred pounds of weight, the balloon jumped into the air like a rocket, and up, up, up we went, over the pine trees and on our way to heaven.

With the speed of the elevated reaction, the instructor started yelling, "Valve, valve, valve!"

Fortunately the valve man knew how much lift would be lost for each second of valving. He opened the helium valves for just enough time to level us off at twenty-five hundred feet. Once leveled, the ride took on a more placid character. The view was beautiful. There was no sound of engines or airflow as we floated along with the wind; it was surprising how far you could hear car horns or dogs barking. Although the temperature was very low, without a wind it was very comfortable.

As we floated along, the instructor now very composed was telling us how this training flight related to an airship that had for some reason lost its propulsion power plants, in other words, its engines. As a floating object we had very limited control over our course, but we did have control over our altitude. By valving helium or dumping weight, we could make our vehicle go up and down. The trick was to control the rate of ascent or descent. This, of course was done with the utmost precision. If you went too high, the helium gas in the balloon would expend and leak out the valve or explode the balloon. If you valved too much helium you would descend too fast and crash. So precision was the key.

As we floated along, the truck below us on the road would follow our flight. The instructor using the megaphone yelled down instructions for the truck driver to turn left or right as we traveled along. From our vantage point we could see the roads better than him. It was surprising how well this maneuver worked.

Finally it was time to demonstrate the landing. I'm sure the other students were thinking the same thing as I was. I hope it won't be as exciting as the take-off.

The instructor gave the order. "Valve ten seconds of helium," he said calmly."

"Aye, aye, sir," said the valve man.

Slowly, ever so slowly we started to descend as the altimeter man announced our altitude every hundred feet. As we descended at what seemed like a reasonable rate of descent, the instructor announced that we would land in a large field about a mile from our position. It looked good to us. What did we know?

As we continued to descend the instructor would ask for varied amounts of valving of helium or discarding of sand to adjust the rate of descent. All was going well. As we approached the parcel of land, which the instructor had selected as our landing, area, we spotted a man standing in the middle of the field. Evidently it was a farmer looking over his frozen patch of ground in preparation for next year's planting.

As we got closer, the instructor, using the megaphone yelled down, "Ahoy farmer."

Well, here was this poor farmer, in the middle of nowhere, and he hears the words 'Ahoy farmer'. You can just imagine his initial reaction. He looked all around as he squatted down to the ground.

"Up here," bellowed the instructor.

That did it. The farmer looked up. What he saw was this large silver round thing descending upon his property. He dropped the stick he had been poking the ground with and ran for the house. As we continued to approach for landing, out of the house he came with the biggest rifle I had ever seen. He stood his ground in front of his house, pointing the rifle up at us. From what we could see he was shaking like a leaf.

In a very high pitched voice the instructor yelled over the megaphone, "Don't shoot, we're friendly."

With the sound of a voice coming from the strange craft in the sky, the farmer held his position, but did not fire.

Again the instructor, "Don't shoot, we're friendly. United States Navy training flight, landing in your area."

With this the farmer lowered his boom buster and started scratching his head. We had all been so involved with the farmer that we forgot about the rate of descent. Down we came with a bang.

Just before landing the instructor did manage to yell, "Bend your knees, we're going to hit hard."

We all squatted down as the basket pounded into the frozen dirt.

The instructor yelled, "Valve, valve, valve!" as we bounced once, twice and finally settle down solid on the surface of the earth.

As we started to climb out of the basket, the instructor advised that we climb out one at a time as helium was valved, to prevent the balloon from going aloft again. So as the valve man continued to valve helium to deflate the balloon we exited the basket one at a time. It seemed that all was going well when one of my fellow students started to holler that he was hurt. He had not heard the instructor say 'bend your knees' prior to landing and he was standing straight up as the basket hit the frozen ground for the first time. He was hurting. With all the clothes we had on, no one knew the extent of his injury at that time.

By the time the truck pulled up to the balloon, we had it almost completely deflated. The farmer was now an honorary member of the deflation crew. He was having the time of his life helping all he could. He even invited all of us into the house for some warm soup. We carried the injured student into the house where he was given much attention by the farmer's wife and two daughters.

After the much needed and appreciated hot soup and admiring attention by the farmer and is family, we loaded the deflated balloon on the stake truck, carried the injured student to the truck cab, and climbed onto the truck bed beside the balloon. One of the students unveiled a bottle of bourbon he had hidden under his coat. We all smiled and looked at the instructor.

"Oh! What the hell," he said, "It's been that kind of day."

Biography of
Glen West

Glen was born in Baltimore, Maryland, grew up in Washington, D.C. and has been writing short stories since third grade. In high school he earned AA for each: U.S. & World Peace, a newspaper for the English tournament era, a play for the Shakespeare era. In the army he served with the Quartermaster Corps, Engineers, and military security at Los Alamos, New Mexico. After attending The George Washington University School of Government, he earned a diploma in Advertising & Marketing from a Philadelphia business school. At the May Company in Washington, he was Assistant Art Director, Production Manager, Art Production Manager and Traffic Coordinator in advertising. For the Washington Post, he processed ads for production, engravers, make-up, and sales. In the following pages are two selections he has written.

GOOD MORNING, DOUGY

Memoir

by Glen West

Douglas B. Weston (that was his formal name, but everyone called him Dougy) awoke early this morning, the sun in his eyes again ever since his parents had moved his bed opposite the window. He had tried talking to them about it, but they would never listen. Pushing his bed himself, he had succeeded in only knocking his pillow to the floor and being scolded for it many times. Oh well, he would try to speak to them about it again. He guessed that's what people meant about not listening to their children, especially three year-olds like him.

He strode to the kitchen, pausing only briefly for a drink; happy his family had water available always. He peered into his parents' room and there they were all snuggled-up together as every morning. Yuck! He reflected, grown-ups sure do get mushy. He preferred to sleep loose in case there was a fire or some other emergency.

Continuing his regular morning tour, he crept up the stairs to the older children's rooms. He had been a latecomer to the family just after they had moved into their new home, and there wasn't room for him upstairs. Beside, Daddy didn't want Mommy to have to climb the stairs to take care of him, even though the kids had insisted upon Dougy being near them. It was just as well, for the kids stayed up too late for Doughy, laughing and playing well beyond their bedtime. Yes, he was well off in the back of the house in his own quiet room, except for that sunrise in his eyes on bright mornings! He would definitely have to broach that subject once more, he decided, as he reached the top of the stairs and ambled into his big sister's room.

Now here was the one girl he loved! Daddy's six year-old sweetness, and his too! He disliked all other girls, for they were always teasing him in the yard, knowing he couldn't climb over the fence. But not his Michele! She always came to play with him first after school, before skipping off to her friends. Her two older brothers dismayed her, but not her little Dougy. She was sleeping sideways, half off her bed, blond hair strung over her pretty young face, one arm dangling to the soft plush carpet barely touching her soft Snoopy doll. Gently he lifted her favorite plaything, nudging it against her until she reached for it, rolled over safely to the middle of her bed cuddling her plush puppy, all the while soundly sleeping!

Next he trekked into his older brothers' room. Kevin was sleeping as always with his legs tangled in his Charlie Brown sheets, feet on his Peanuts pillow, thumb in mouth! That boy! He's going to wear braces if I don't keep helping him, though Doughy, as he nudged Kev's elbow and the eight year old reached to cover himself, legs untangled, thumb removed! Dougy withdrew cautiously from Kev's bed, as one time he had tripped over the baseball, which rolled into the bat that fell, causing the football and basket ball to roll out of the room bouncing loudly against the hall wall and thundering down the stairs! Doughy had escaped with his life, as the whole household had been aroused! Kevin was obviously not the very tidy sportsman of the family.

Michael, ten this summer, was the electronics genius of the family. Last time Dougy had turned the knob on Mike's hand built intercom, filling the house with loud rock and roll at six in the morning! He had escaped to his security blanket! This time he left his big brother undisturbed!

Having completed his morning ritual, Dougy leaped down the stairs, but not quietly enough, for he heard his Daddy shout, "That Dougy! He's up too early again! What's wrong with that boy?"

"You're right, Honey," his Mommy, replied sleepily, "The sunrise reached his eyes. You'll have to move his bed back to where it was, first thing!"

Dougy smiled as he darted through the house and outside to a beautiful spring morning. Robins were singing as he dashed merrily to beneath his favorite weeping willow, ears flapping in the breeze, barking playfully as the robins took wing. It was going to be a beautiful day for a happy Beagle!

BED AND BREAKFAST CAT AND ZAK

"What was that noise? Was it in the kitchen? Hello, I'm Jericho, the bed and breakfast cat." I open one eye, as is my usual custom, to survey the situation. Nothing amiss. It is my responsibility to guard the most important room in this establishment: the kitchen, of course. Harboring all those good things to eat. Already my mouth is watering just thinking about them. "Wait! There's that clatter again!" I open my other eye. "Maybe, I'm missing something! No, I'm right!" I'm scurrying to my kitchen. "Meow! Intruders!"

"Hey, where did that darn cat come from? He'll wake the household! Grab him! Throw him into the meat locker!" the male intruder exclaims.

Before I know what is happening and can jump aside, I'm grabbed by the female accomplice, "Meow."

"Ow! That darn cat scratched me!" she screams, and rightly so, for I am digging my claws in as deep as I can into her arm in which she is crushing me. But before I can extricate myself from this dangerous situation, she hurls me far back to the rear of the meat locker. At once, even before I hit the rear wall, I am literally flying through the air, racing for the door. "Bang!" Too late! It slams shut! I immediately jump as high as I can to reach the door lever. "Clink" goes the latch. I'm trapped inside the meat locker! I can't escape. I'll freeze to death! "Grr!" I'm shivering! Already icicles are forming on my ears and eyelids!

"Zak! Zak," can he hear me through the massive door? "Zak, Zak I'm locked in the freezer!"

"What was that? I'm Zak, the snoot-nosed hound, guardian of that most important front entrance to this bed and breakfast establishment. No body, but no body gets by me! "Growl." I open one eye, a habit I acquired from that darn milk-sucking kitchen guardian cat, Jericho.

"What's going on in there? What's he up to now? It's not even dawn!" I lift myself slowly, ears as long as my snoot-nose, slapping the carpet. Big yawn! I can hear a faint meow coming from the kitchen. "What more trouble is that cursed Jericho into this time? Well let me see! Hey, his milk and water dishes are knocked over! What a mess! He's in real trouble this time! Wait! All the kitchen drawers are open! Look there are raw meat scars leading to the outside door! There's been a real calamity here! Jericho! Jericho! Where are you? Troublesome cat."

"Zak! Zak! I'm right here. Locked in the meat locker! I'm freezing in here!" I shake more icicles from my back and tail, "Get me out of here, Zak!"

"What are you doing in there, Jericho. Didn't our masters serve you enough fish to suit your fancy?"

"You scrawny kitchen mongrel! Just lift the inside lever and get me out of here before we wake all the guests!"

"I can't reach it, Zak! Help me."

"What happened here? How did you get locked in there in the first place, Jericho!"

"The robbers locked me in here, Zak!"

"The robbers?" I questioned. "Robbers!" I bellow, as I jump as high as I can to reach the outside latch to release my stranded freezing friend. "I can't lift the latch with me teeth or paws! We need help!"

I start barking a mean streak as I hear Jericho's loud screeching meows through the dense heavy door.

The chaotic uproar awakens the housemasters. "What's going on downstairs? Zak is barking like thunder and Jericho's meows are shrieking. Are those two fighting again at this hour? It's not even dawn!"

"You better go down and see," the housemistress replies. "I've never heard them so vociferous. They're frightened about something. Be careful!"

Upon reaching the kitchen, the master asks, "Zak, what's happened here? This place is a mess." Looking around, he adds, "and where is Jericho?"

Jumping frantically against the locker door, I bark, "Jericho's locked in the freezer!"

"Alright, Zak, let me reach the lever." As he unlatches the door, Jericho bursts out, shivering, coat covered with frost.

"Oh! You poor little kitty, all wet and cold; here, let me warm you," cries the housemistress, having just arrived in time.

She picks me up, fondles and strokes my poor shivering, almost frozen body. "Purr, purr," I sob smirking at Zak.

"How do you like that? I saved his scrawny milk-sucking mangy, frostbitten good-for-nothing alley cat and he gets all the attention. I'm out of here!" Head high, tail up, I march haughtily to my bed, sulking.

"Zak! Good Boy! Well done! You're a hero," exclaims the housemaster.

I turn at once, tail wagging smartly, eyes beaming, barking repeatedly. "Yes, you're right. I Zak am a hero! I agree." As he stoops to me nose-to-nose, eyes-to-eyes, shaking my paws.

"Meow! I Jericho agree profoundly. We are partner guardians of this bed and breakfast."

"Wolf! I Zak consent intensely," getting in the last word.

Biography of
Allen Watkins

Allen Watkins was born in rural USA (Neodesha, Kansas) during the 30s. He attended public schools there, graduating from High School in 1953. After one semester at the University of Wichita in Wichita, Kansas, Allen went to work for Boeing Aircraft Company in Wichita to earn money to continue his education but never returned to school. He was drafted into the Army in 1956 but was released early because of a bad back. Allen was employed by Northrop Grumman in St Augustine, Florida in 1985. He worked for them until his retirement in 2001.

After moving to The Villages, Florida, Allen joined the Creative Writers group. He also joined The Villages Theater Company. Allen tried out for a part in the play, "All Because of Agatha" and got a part as Flip Cannon, reporter.

Allen writes poetry for the International War Veterans Poetry Archives; honoring veterans that have served this country. He has had poems published in "Distant Echoes", a printed journal for and about veterans of all wars. Allen is writing a fiction novel about an English boy in the 1700s.

THEY WERE THERE

Poem

by Allen Watkins

I saw old men and women at a war memorial this day.
They wore no uniforms or medals but I could hear them say.
"I was there at Pearl Harbor; God how did I survive?
So many friends that were there are now no longer alive."
There, that old timer with a cane, walking through the mall;
He has memory of D-day and the beach named Omaha.
This group of men was sub mariners and served under the sea.
They call themselves Sea Dragons; a name I truly believe.
The old Korean veteran said, "they didn't call it a war; yet –
So many men were killed there, what were they fighting for?"
"Were you country?" Asked the Viet Nam vet.
A nod would suffice; nothing else needed to be said.
They were there and they remember but their thoughts are for younger men.
For they have children and grandchildren now fighting on foreign land.
They never felt as powerless as they do this day,
Ask and they would pick up arms again and enter in the fray.
Oh, they were there thank God, when their country was against the wall.
But it's time to pass the torch to others that have answered to the call.
I can only stand in awe for the heroes that abound.
They are just gentle men, well known in their hometown.
Now they can only pray for those in service quest; but –
The younger ones will join them after giving it their best.
If you ever see a war memorial and you should wander near,
You might hear a younger man say, "Yes, I was there."

Biography of
Ancella Bickley

Ancella Radford Bickley is a native of West Virginia. The writer's group call her 'Cill' and recognize her as the most prolific and professional writer in town. She holds a Bachelor of Arts Degree from Virginia State College, magna cum laude and graduate degrees from Marshall University and West Virginia University.

Cill's professional experiences include teaching in public schools and at the college level. She also served as a college administrator, although her particular interest has been black history of West Virginia about which she has written extensively.

She is currently engaged in developing a collection of stories based upon people and incidents and the sense of place so vital to Appalachians. In 2001, her story "Martha" was published by the Jesse Stuart Foundation in a book entitled "Appalachian Love Stories."

For Eva Ledbetter whose story this is.

THE BATTLE OF THE BOTTLE

Fiction

Ancella R. Bickley

Eleven-year-old Fannie stopped for a minute outside of the door of the room where Granddaddy and Big Momma slept. She could hear the soft murmur of their voices as they said their morning prayers. She knew if she were to go in, Big Momma would scoot over and make a place between her and Granddaddy so that Fannie could kneel with them at the side of their bed. If she woke early on school mornings, Fannie usually went in their room. She didn't really pray, but she liked to be sandwiched between Granddaddy and Big Momma. Big Momma would reach her comforting brown arm around Fannie, hugging as she prayed, and that gave Fannie a happy feeling to start the day with.

This morning was different though. As much as she would like to be with Big Momma, Fannie had something else to do. She had some thinking and planning and work to do before Aunt Kate got up. Closing the door softly so that she wouldn't awaken anyone, she let herself out of the house with her bottle in one hand. Aunt Kate and Dear had been home for just a few days and hadn't gotten back in the swing of the early rising that was usual on the farm. Big Momma never woke them. She was just so glad that her daughters still wanted to spend their summer vacations at home on the farm that she never asked anything of them.

They always said the same thing when they came home. "Teaching's hard, Momma. City kids are not like country kids. They're harder to deal with. It's wonderful to have a chance to rest – to be back here with you and Daddy and Fannie."

Big Momma's face would light up and Fannie knew that she was thinking about making pound cake or homemade ice cream or some treat that Dear and Aunt Kate would like.

Dear. That dumb new kid in Fannie's class had a hard time understanding that Dear was her mother and that Big Momma was her grandmother. "I used to call my Mom 'Mother Dear' when I was little," Fannie had explained about Dear. "Then I decided that was too long and I'd just say 'Dear'. My Mom's real name is Marie King and mine is Fannie King, and Big Momma and Granddaddy are Mr. & Mrs. Mathews and my Aunt Kate is Kathryn Matthews and my Daddy doesn't live with us and my Granddaddy grows tobacco." She's just decided to tell all about the family at one time. That way that dumb kid wouldn't keep asking her stuff.

Fannie and Jane Long from two farms over were the only two black kids in the school. None of the teachers were black, even Aunt Kate and Dear went away to get jobs after they finished college. They only got to come home at vacation time and during the summer. Most of the rest of the time just Fannie and Big Momma and Granddaddy were together. Being on the farm was fun except for the snakes. Now and then a black snake got in the house. One even got into a suitcase one time and when Fannie opened it to pack for a visit to Dear and Aunt Kate, the snake just came crawling out. Fannie yelled and started running out of the room. Big Momma was laying her clothes out on the bed to put in the suitcase and turned around just as the snake was crawling back into the dark closet. She told Fannie to go and get Granddaddy while she watched to see where the snake went. Granddaddy came running in with a croaker sack and the rake. He pulled the snake out of the closet and grabbed him behind the head and put him in the croaker sack and took him out of the house.

"They won't hurt you," Granddaddy told her. "They're as afraid of you as you are of them, and they help to keep the mice away."

Ugh! Fannie shivered remembering.

Standing in front of the big barn door, she pushed it open and went in. She stopped for a minute waiting for her eyes to get accustomed to the dimness, smelling the combined odors of straw and animals, and searching for any movement that might indicate a snake. It kind of stunk, but it didn't stink, she thought. She wouldn't want to smell it all the time, but a little now and then wasn't too bad. She went up to Bitsy and patted her on the side while she looked around for the stool to sit on. Filling her bottle with milk was her regular morning ritual. Her Granddaddy had taught her to milk as soon as her hands were big enough to fit around the cow's teats. This was probably the last time this summer that she could fill her bottle directly from the cow because Aunt Kate would be fussing with her as soon as she had rested some. After this morning, Fannie would fill her bottle from the milk that Big Momma already had in the refrigerator and would spend her summer sneaking it out somewhere to suck on it. It was like hide and seek, and she would spend half her time thinking about how to keep Aunt Kate from finding her while she sucked it.

"Nice Bitsy. I love you Bitsy," she crooned as she seated herself on the stool and reached for the teat. "Good Bitsy." She leaned her forehead against the cow's side as she directed the flow of milk into the narrow opening of the bottle. Squeeze and release. Squeeze and release. It only took a few minutes to fill the bottle. "Thanks, Bitsy." She stood up, patted Bitsy on the side, moved the stool back behind the bale of hay where Granddaddy kept it and walked out of the barn being careful not to spill any of the milk in the bottle.

In the kitchen, Fannie strained the milk into another bottle, turned the nipple upside down in the bottle, put the little round cap on it and screwed the ring around the outside. She stopped and listened for a minute. Her Aunt Kate was still asleep. Now where could she hide the bottle where Aunt Kate couldn't find it?

Last night while she was helping Big Momma clear the table, she heard Aunt Kate and Dear talking about the bottle, so she knew that she was going to have a hard time with Aunt Kate this summer. It was a game they played. Last summer when Aunt Kate was at home, Fannie had found all kinds of places to suck her bottle; she had hidden behind the woodpile, locked herself in the bathroom, and even crawled under Big Momma's high four poster bed.

Aunt Kate had been fussing about the bottle a long time. "I'm going to let you get away with it now," Aunt Kate said when she came home for the Easter vacation, "But when I come home this summer, I'm going to wean you from that thing."

"Momma lets her do it, Kate," Dear told her. "She says it comforts Fannie and doesn't hurt anybody."

"Comfort! Comfort! How in the world can you agree that an eleven year old needs the comfort of sucking a bottle! I never heard of anything so ridiculous, Marie. Would you want your class of fifth graders sitting around with baby bottles in their mouths?" Aunt Kate said raising her voice slightly.

"Well, Fannie doesn't really sit around with the bottle in her mouth, Kate. She just does it in the evening when she gets home from school or when she watches television after supper during the summer time."

"I don't care when she does it. That girl's eleven years old and sucking a bottle is for babies. You and Momma can't make up for your not being here by keeping her a baby and letting her suck a bottle forever."

"Um," Fannie heard Dear say. Dear and Aunt Kate never really fussed with each other.

The talk about Fannie's bottle was about as much of a disagreement as they ever had.

Standing by the kitchen sink, Fannie turned the bottle upside down and shook it to see if any of the milk would leak out. The top was on good and tight. She decided to take the bottle down in the cellar and put it in the old refrigerator that Big Momma used to keep the extra vegetables in. If she put the bottle way in the back behind the vegetables, she didn't think her Aunt Kate would bother to move the vegetables to look for it. At least, she won't do it today, Fannie thought. Today Aunt Kate will still be too tired to hunt very hard.

Fannie opened the cellar door and pulled the string that turned on the light at the top of the steps. There was another string at the bottom of the steps for the light near the refrigerator. She reached up and grabbed it as she came down the last step, then opened the refrigerator and moving the pokes of vegetables aside, she hid the bottle of milk back in the corner of the bottom shelf and then packed the vegetables in front of it. She had just gotten back upstairs and closed the door to the cellar when Big Momma came into the kitchen.

"Morning, Honey. How about some breakfast with Granddaddy?"

"I think I'll just have this orange and wait for Dear and Aunt Kate to get up," Fannie replied, taking an orange from the dish of fruit on the kitchen table.

"All right," Big Momma told her. "I'm going to make bacon and eggs for him, but when the girls come down, we'll do something special like making waffles." And with a rattle of pots and pans, she set about making breakfast for her husband.

Fannie went into the living room and turned on the TV. She peeled the orange and made a little pile of rind on the glass top of the coffee table in front of her. She was finishing the orange and watching Mr. Rogers when Aunt Kate and her mother came down the steps. Both were wearing flowered housecoats. Dear came over and sat down beside her taking one of her hands in hers.

"Hey, girl," Aunt Kate said, and coming up behind Fannie she caught her top braid, pulled her head back, and bent over and placed a kiss on Fannie's smooth brown forehead. "Where is it?" and she moved the pillow beside Fannie, grinning as she felt beneath it.

"Where's what?" Fannie asked, as if she didn't know.

"You know. The thing that starts with a 'B'," Aunt Kate grinned at her.

"I haven't got it," Fannie replied, knowing that Aunt Kate was teasing and the serious hunt wasn't going to begin for a while.

"Well, I need my coffee. How about you, Marie? Want some of Momma's good coffee?"

"You know I do," Dear said. "I been waiting all year for this," and she kissed Fannie on the cheek and got up and followed Aunt Kate into the kitchen.

Fannie could hear bits of the conversation as the cups rattled and the smell of coffee drifted through the door.

"I don't want to interfere with Momma's rules, Kate," she heard Dear say in between the sound of chairs being dragged from under the kitchen table. "After all, Momma's got the day to day responsibility of Fannie. I'm just here during summers and vacations. It's what Momma says that counts."

"You just don't want to come down on her when you're here, Marie. I think you've got a case of the guilties."

Fannie moved to where she could see in the kitchen and hear the talk a little better. She had to know how serious Aunt Kate was about her bottle so she could figure out how to protect it.

From her viewing spot in the living room, Fannie squirmed and waited for her mother's reply to Aunt Kate.

"Well, I guess that I do worry about not being with Fannie more. Even if it's your own mother raising your child, you worry about not being there."

"I knew it," Aunt Kate said. "I just wanted to hear you say so."

"Momma, I know why Marie doesn't take that bottle away from Fannie, but what about you. Why do you let her keep it?"

"It makes Fannie happy, Kate," her mother told her, closing the top on the waffle iron and standing for a moment to watch it steam around the edges.

"But don't you think something's wrong about a big girl like Fannie sucking a bottle?" Aunt Kate wanted to know.

"Wrong?" Fannie saw Big Momma turn toward Aunt Kate, spatula in her hand. "Wrong for me, Kate, is when you hurt other people. Fannie don't do none a that. She's a good girl. She don't fight and she makes good grades and is respectful to me and her Granddaddy and her teachers, and she gets along all right with the other children. So I can't use 'wrong' when I talk about her."

"Oh, Momma, you know what I mean," Aunt Kate said going over to Big Momma and putting her arms around her. "You know how much I love Fannie and what a fine girl I think she is. Maybe 'wrong' wasn't the right word. Help me, Marie. You're the English teacher. Help me find a word," and Aunt Kate turned and looked at Dear, arms still around Big Momma.

Don't do it, Dear, Fannie thought, looking in her mother's direction then closing her eyes while she sent the message. That's what the kids at school called sending shinies. Shinies were like waving and smiling to somebody across the room. Only at Fannie's school you didn't wave and smile or say anything. You looked hard at them when they weren't watching and sent a message from your head to theirs. Almost all of the time they would look up and see you and smile at you – sending you some shinies in return. Fannie had first heard about shinies after one of the older kids came from summer vacation talking about a smiley church service that she'd gone to when she went to see her family in another state. She changed it from smilies to shinies and showed some of them how it worked. Soon everybody started doing it. Now it was just a regular thing in their school.

"I'm not even going to think about it," Dear told Aunt Kate. "I'm just glad to be home and I'm going to sit here and enjoy Momma's good food and coffee and love all of y'all and not worry about Fannie's bottle."

"Well, I'm going to sit her with you, Marie, and do the same thing, but that's just because I'm still tired. As soon as I rest up some, I'm going to break her of that bottle if it's the last thing that I do."

Out in the living room, Fannie grinned to herself and moved back on the couch and started looking at TV again. He bottle was safe for the time being.

As the days passed, however, the battle heated up. Just in case Aunt Kate found the bottle that she was using, Fannie had bought a couple of extra ones when she and Big Momma went to the drugstore in town. Good thing, too. She made the mistake of leaving one of the plastic bottles in the kitchen one morning and Aunt Kate got it and stuck holes in it with the ice pick. She dropped one of the glass ones on the sidewalk and broke it one day when Aunt Kate was chasing her. She sort of deserved to lose that one because she was teasing Aunt Kate by sucking it in front of her. After that, she'd sneak in the kitchen and fill her bottle whenever she could. She lost another one when Aunt Kate discovered her hiding place in the refrigerator in the root cellar, so she couldn't hide it there anymore. And since the weather was getting so hot, she couldn't leave the bottle out of the refrigerator too long or the milk would sour. Out smarting Aunt Kate was getting harder and harder.

It was the psychological warfare that was the worst, though. Aunt Kate had a picture of Fannie sucking her bottle and she took it to town and had it enlarged to poster size. She scotch taped it to the ceiling of the kitchen. It was out of Fannie's reach even with the ladder, so Fannie just had to look at it. She couldn't talk Dear or her Granddaddy into taking it down. They said that the fight was between Fannie and Aunt Kate and they were just neutral spectators and couldn't help either side. Granddaddy had a chalk board on the back porch and he'd keep the score of what he called "The Battle of the Bottle."

Aunt Kate got a point for the poster. Most of the time Fannie could ignore the poster, but as she sat having her morning cereal and looking up at it, she had to admit that she did look kind of silly sucking the bottle with one hand and twirling her top pigtail with the other.

Dear talked Aunt Kate into taking the poster down when company was coming. She didn't think that interfered with her being neutral. She told Aunt Kate that she was just protecting her baby a bit. "It'll embarrass her too much, Kate. You don't really want to do that, do you?"

"Sure I do," Aunt Kate said. But she took the poster down anyway. Granddaddy had a hard time figuring whether or not to give a point for that. When he finally decided to give one to Fannie, her aunt got a little miffed and Fannie giggled.

To pay her back and get some points, her Aunt Kate made a big rag doll and sat it in the rocking chair in the living room with a cardboard bottle up to its mouth and a sign saying, "Fannie."

Fannie would steal the sign and the bottle. Granddaddy would up her score whenever she took them, but Aunt Kate would just put other on the doll. She must have made a dozen of those things, Fannie thought.

Dear talked Aunt Kate out of putting the sign and bottle on the doll when the church circle met at their house., The ladies loved the rag doll and wanted Aunt Kate to make them some so that they could sell them at the Christmas Bazaar.

"I call it my Fannie doll," Aunt Kate told them, putting her arm around Fannie as Fannie stood beside her holding the tray while Aunt Kate served the ladies their coffee. Aunt Kate chuckled while she said it, and even Big Momma had that look in her eyes that let Fannie know she was laughing inside. Dear just looked funny. Fannie felt betrayed – like Big Momma and Dear were siding with Aunt Kate.

Fannie had planned what she would do if Aunt Kate told the ladies the rest of it – about the doll's bottle and about her bottle. She was going to drop the tray and make such a mess that Aunt Kate would have to stop talking to clean it up.

But Aunt Kate never said anything. Fannie heaved a sigh of relief when they finished with the tray and took it to the kitchen.

Aunt Kate hugged her and Fannie hugged her back. "We still love each other, don't we, Fan?"

"Sure," Fannie said, thinking all the while that this was a good time to suck her bottle while Aunt Kate was busy with the church ladies.

Keeping on with the bottle was tougher than Fannie thought it was going to be.

After a while, Aunt Kate started offering her things to quit. And every time Fannie said "no." Aunt Kate would offer something bigger. Fannie turned down a new bike, but almost wavered when Aunt Kate offered to get her ears pierced and buy her some gold earrings. Some of the girls at school were beginning to wear earrings, and Fannie had been eyeing them longingly for the last year. But it was when Aunt Kate began talking about a trip to Disneyland that Fannie started thinking seriously about giving up her bottle. She started tapering off. She wouldn't have a bottle everyday, but she made her aunt think that she did. Pretty soon, Fannie knew that she could quit if she wanted to.

One day, in the late summer, Fannie fixed her bottle and hid it behind the woodpile. Her aunt had been watching her pretty closely, but Fannie planned to drink the bottle when Aunt Kate went to the bathroom. They were all sitting on the front porch and as soon as her Aunt Kate got up to go in the house, Fannie went racing around the house to the woodpile. She knew that her aunt would be gone a good while because she took a magazine with her. When Fannie got to the woodpile and moved the logs away, she looked down and started to scream. There was a big black snake wrapped around the bottle. Fannie jumped back. Startled, the snake moved away from the bottle and burrowed deep into the woodpile. Fannie stood there shaking and crying. After a few minutes, she dried her eyes and went back around to the front porch. Dear was sitting in the swing stringing beans. Fannie moved the poke out of her mother's lap and said, "Dear, will you hold me a little bit."

"Of course, honey," her mother replied and put her arms around Fannie and pulled her close. They were sitting that way when Aunt Kate came back out on the porch.

"How about that Disneyland trip?" Fannie asked her Aunt Kate.

"You mean you quit?" Aunt Kate wanted to know.

"Yes,' Fannie answered.

"I won! I won! I wore her down." Aunt Kate grabbed Fannie and kissed her and went running around the house to write "WINNER" in big letters on her side of the chalkboard.

They had a great time at Disneyland the next summer. Fannie never told Aunt Kate about the snake.

Biography of
Joe Thek

Dr. Joe Thek is a retired physician. He came to the Villages from Scranton, Pennsylvania, where he worked as an Emergency Room physician. Now retired, he is presently writing a novel COSMIC SOUL EXCHANGE that he shares with the Writers' Group. Joe writes everything from human interest to adventure stories, even romantic ones. His fellow writers love his sly sense of humor and the knowledge that he works diligently and long hours on his new craft.

A graduate of Rutgers University, as a young man he enjoyed athletic activities and mountain climbing while studying to become a doctor, even afterwards when he had time. Now he devotes most of his extra hours to writing. Joe has three children and one grandchild. A finished novel NO EXIT is presently in the hands of a publisher.

THE MIRACLE OF ST. ROSE

Fiction

by Joe Thek

St. Rose's high school and parish were in Riverside, New Jersey. People often claimed it was in need of a miracle. The roof of the church leaked more than secrets from the U.S. State Department. But at least the drips didn't have lead in them like the tap water did. It was only usable in the baptismal font, and then, only if you didn't dunk the baby.

Then, too, the walls of the high school were asbestos-lined and would be condemned if not replaced within the year. The most regular parishioners were the termites who had been eating the choir loft for Christmas and Easter dinners since 1950. But rumor had it that they weren't Catholics at all since they continued to gnaw away right through Lent. The walls needed Tom Sawyer's brush, the ceiling, Michelangelo's.

The parish was dying a natural death but for Father Paul, Congressman Ned Kane, Mother Veronica, sophomore Frank and his freshman brother, Jerry McAllister, and the strange events of April 8th, 1965. Maybe Jupiter was aligned with Mars. Maybe the Furies were making a comeback. Or maybe, just maybe, it was a miracle.

On that morning, the priest's round, mild face peeped through his bedroom curtains and looked out upon the church grounds behind the rectory. In the early morning fog, he dimly saw the outlines of tents, covered booths, and the platform for the band. The Ferris wheel, assembled the day before, loomed over the bazaar like a patron saint. Its steel cylinders rose powerfully from the ground only to be lost in the low lying mist as if they were reaching up to God and heaven and were ready to take anybody there if the person liked. Father Paul lost several nights' sleep wondering if the wheel would be built on time. Now his only concern was the weather.

If that sun burns off the fog like it's supposed to, we'll be all right. Everything's ready. By tonight, we'll be out of debt.

Having grown up in the town, he was well aware of the desperate shape of St. Rose's when the priest became pastor. But, it was a challenge. If he could turn this parish around, his reputation as a financial wizard would be assured. But, first Father Paul needed to prove to the archdiocese that he had learned the first law of the priesthood – to raise money and lots of it – by rescuing St. Rose's from ruin. Father Paul was determined to take a true accounting of every soul in the parish.

So, our young priest spent months studying the traditional methods of fleecing the flock. It was obvious Sunday collections weren't ever enough. Of course, there were the weddings, baptisms, and funerals, but it seemed the sacraments just weren't as marketable as they once were. Although the Church had perfected ways to create profit from any arrival or departure as well as any airline, the competition became stiff since the deregulation of the Reformation. He knew that heretics were bad for business unless you could burn a few of them and charge admission.

With attendance down, new methods of raising revenues were devised. Selling indulgences and simony were tapped out like the Athenian silver mines at Laurium. Even those modern innovations like Bingo had not taken the parish out of the red.

So the good Father decided upon a more flamboyant entertainment. A bazaar, complete with local culinary delight, a fortuneteller, belly dancer, games of chance and rides, bribed the lost souls into coming to the church grounds. A rock band attracted the enormous disposable income of the younger generation.

The beauty of it all was the priest literally got all of the participants to volunteer for a "song and a prayer". Indulgences couldn't be sold, but there was no rule about barter. So, Father Paul promised everyone to use his influence to help free one poor soul – of their choice – from Purgatory for each person that gave their services freely.

Congressman Ned Kane was the consummate politician. Having been a trial lawyer for fifteen years, he learned that verdicts had very little to do with true guilt or innocence. Rather, Ned conspired to impress the jury with his meticulous appearance and eloquence, and the judge with his strict adherence to procedure. He never impressed them with the truth. Like Demosthenes, Kane formed opinions in others by distorting facts. To him, truth was irrelevant. Winning was the game. And so, he entered politics.

To the Congressman, an election was an inconvenient means to an end. But he did believe strongly in democracy. Under what other system could a relatively obscure man from a poor background seek and gain power? All one needed was the cunning of Richard Nixon and the organization of Richard Daley – and a rich wife. The beauty of the system was Ned got the consent of the governed. When he told the correct lies and bribed the right people, Kane might even become a senator. With a true Machiavellian spirit, he knew one must be willing to do anything to win. Anything. It wouldn't matter to him if every one of his constituents silently hated him. Their opinion meant nothing.

If they had any sense at all, would they ever elect a man like me?

But Ned Kane was, incongruously, an ardent Catholic as well. As all people are fusions of contradictions, so too was the Congressman. Almost every Saturday afternoon, after golf, of course, he confessed his political crimes with his less frequent sins of passion to the kindly Father Paul. Ned gained absolution, then abstained from sin long enough to receive Communion on Sunday morning. Come Monday, and sometimes even Sunday night, he began the cycle again by returning to his inveterate scheming ways. Despite the priest's constant advice to mend his ways, the Congressman had behaved in such a manner since the beginning of his political career.

On that morning, Kane was visiting home as he did every spring and summer weekend. His alleged motive for this weekly exodus from D.C. was to keep in touch with his constituents. But the real reason was to play golf at the club, and then, to confession.

Frank knew the week before the bazaar that somehow he'd be getting punished with another weekend detention. Whenever Mother Veronica needed help around the school, or Father Paul around the church, Frank was sure to get caught doing something even when he wasn't, like the first detention from the high school principal earlier in his sophomore year.

"And what would you like to do when you grow up?" the hard-of-hearing fiftyish Mother Veronica asked him in class.

The question seemed relatively innocuous. However, the nun wasn't wearing her hearing aid because Billy Westbrook brought a dog whistle to class for weeks and blew it whenever Mother Veronica turned away. Of course, no one could hear it. No one, but her. She'd fumble with her hearing aid as if the battery was bad. Finally, Mother Veronica removed it all together.

"I'd like playing the French horn," Frank answered facetiously.

He didn't know it, but that's not what she heard.

I'd like laying a French whore, is what it sounded like to her.

Now, Frank couldn't know the good sister's thoughts. If he could, Frank might have trembled to embark on such a perilous and harrowing journey through the twisted labyrinth leading to the grim dungeons of Mother Veronica's mind. In the future, he learned that the kindling for the Inferno consists of twigs named "superstition" and "intolerance" in 157 different languages.

The nun's face looked like the Soviet flag complete with hammer and sickle. Her right hand twitched as she tried to control anger. Memories of having boys stand on their heads in the corner, or of locking them in the cloakroom, flitted through her mind. Mother Veronica could feel the three-sided ruler she used to strike knuckles. But, gone were the good old days. Corporal punishment was frowned upon now. Mother Veronica would never have become a nun in the first place if she knew force couldn't be used to discipline students. Inflicting pain and terror was half the ball game.

The other half was sex. Mother Veronica detested any mention of it. In every waking moment, she felt its innuendo, its pulsing, subconscious, control of man's soul. Every dome was a woman's breast, every pointed object a penis, and every hole, a vagina. The nun couldn't bring herself to eat carrots or bananas, unless they were sliced first. She nearly worshiped the typewriter because it had liberated her from the bondage of the pen and pencil, their very names revealing their erotic origin. Yes, Mother Veronica was a Freudian at heart. There was nothing she was more proud of than her ongoing conquest of her own sexuality. It was a struggle no doubt.

For years, Mother Veronica grew weak and sweaty whenever she saw the boys in their gym uniforms. Many of the priests the nun worked with thought her to be an asthmatic because she was always short winded whenever they came near. However, if anyone were attracted to her, it would have been considered a miracle, a proof of God's intervention and temporary abrogation of the natural law. With Mother Veronica's whiskers and moustache, crossed eyes and pockmarked face, only a blind man, or a priest, could have possibly been attracted to her.

She knew every boy thought about "laying a French whore" because the nun thought so often about being one herself. But to brazenly admit it! Mother Veronica had overcome the temptation, and she would teach Frank to do the same. The nun didn't care if she was reprimanded by the order.

Whap! Went her hand across his bewildered face.

"Don't you ever say such a thing again!" Mother Veronica barked. Sexual demons like Don Quixote's windmills appeared before her eyes, and she thrust a penile lance at them.

Whoosh! Struck the backhand against the teen's cheek.

"But . . . ."

"No butts, or breasts or kisses either! Three weeks detention."

Frank was a favorite child. Admired for his health, he was the best representative his mother would ever give to posterity. But far beyond that, was the resemblance Frank bore her. He was dark skinned, with black, straight hair and brown eyes, like her. However, beauty in a woman can sometimes be transformed into coarseness in her son.

Although he was obviously her child, Frank's eyes were deeper set, nose broader, and as he grew, his lips curled almost imperceptibly in what appeared to be a perpetual mocking smile. Frank was far from handsome. Yet, his face held an attraction akin to beauty, as if it were a counterfeit reflection of hers. But, she was blind to all that.

His real interest was electronics. Everyone knew he was a genius with wires and sound systems. It was that interest that got him his latest detention.

The sophomore sex education class was that week. As usual, the girls and boys were separated with Mother Veronica giving the females their lecture, while the priest gave the males theirs.

Frank told Jerry he wanted to share the nun's lecture with everyone else in the school. The teen compared it to the Sermon on the Mount.

"Don't you think it would have been great if someone wired the mount so everyone could hear?"

"We'll get detention," his brother noted.

"We're gonna get it anyway. Father needs help at the bazaar. Might as well be for something good. Come on; it'll be fun, and you can always go to confession later."

Jerry finally agreed. With his help, Frank hooked up a microphone to the P.A. system. When Mother Veronica began talking about copulation, he switched the receiver on and the sister's rasping voice was broadcast in every room in the school.

"Now girls, what I'm going to describe now is truly disgusting, and I know it will make you wonder how any self-respecting woman could ever let herself get into such a mess. The whole problem with sex is the men. You see, they have – urges."

The word reverberated through the school like a clap of thunder.

'Urges,' the younger brother thought. *'That's why I'm rambunctious with girls. It's not my fault at all; it's those old "urges" again.'*

"That's all they want from a girl," the nun continued. "They want to put their love member in your love member and . . . and . . . copulate. **Cop-u-late!** I know you want to put your hands over your ears, and wish you'd never heard that word. But, you have to hear it, or else some boy will come along and take advantage of you. Don't ever forget that, girls. If you do, you'll ruin your life."

Monique Montmarquet, a buxom lass, who was nicknamed "Frenchy" for more than one reason, asked, "But sex isn't always bad, is it Mother?"

"Sex before marriage is always evil; even after it connubial bliss is only allowed for the sake of children."

'*Thank God for children,*' Jerry thought.

"It's never to be used for pleasure. Ever! If it is, then women become like men. Animals! Slaves of sex and Satan! It's a sin. That's why Christ was born of a virgin birth. God could never be brought into the world as a result of that wicked desire."

"But can't a woman love a man?" Frenchy asked, undaunted.

"Love! You mean lust, don't you?"

Mother Veronica was almost wheezing.

By now, all the other classes in the school were in an uproar, and Father Paul knew exactly who to blame.

"I should get both of you expelled for this," he told the brothers. "But instead I'm going to give you a chance to redeem yourselves."

'*Here it comes,*' Frank thought. '*Weekend detention. I wonder what he wants me to do now.*'

"Since you're such a whiz with electronics," the priest continued, "I'm going to let you do all the wiring for the bazaar. You can think of it as a penance. And you'd better do it right, or else you'll be spending every weekend from now until graduation in detention:

After school, he and Jerry walked home together. "I'm sick of being their damn slave labor," Frank stated angrily. "I'm gonna get him this time."

The fog disappeared before noon. The brothers were already busy; with amplifiers, speakers, and wiring for the stage.

"Come on, Jerry; we have to get this stuff done."

"What's your hurry?"

"Wait 'till you see what I've got planned for later."

"Look, I don't want any more trouble. Dad is about ready to kill me for not being home to do the yard work as it is. And Mom, well, you know how she is whenever we get detention"

"Don't worry about Mom. I'll take the blame. This is gonna be the best prank we've ever pulled."

"Better than the X-rated movie at the CCD class?"

"Yup. Father Paul is never gonna mess with us again."

The bazaar opened as scheduled at two. The priest blessed people at the entrance. By three o'clock, hundreds of people young and old arrived and Father Paul was sure of a success. He sauntered from Mr. Gianelli's pizzas to Mrs. Krywicki's kielbasa, and the priest grew fatter by the hour. The music of change being spent on counter tops pleased him even if it was for belly dancers and palm readers.

One of the more popular booths was the one featuring Frenchy Montmarquet, serving a detention herself, yielding kisses for fifty cents. It was adjacent to the stage where the brothers were just finishing the electrical work. The rear of the booth was open, and Jerry could see her leaning over the counter top on her elbows with buttocks wiggling behind in tight jeans.

"Geez, she's not wearing any underwear!" he noticed, unable to take his eyes off her.

"Jerry! Keep your mind on business," Frank chided him.

"Will you look at that! I think I love her!"

"Remember what Mother Veronica said. I thought you were a good Catholic," he stated.

"I am. I can't help it. It's the 'urges'. I'll go to confession later."

"Come on. I have something to explain to you."

The younger brother, keeping one eye on Frenchy, responded, "Shoot."

Frank took a small wireless receiver out of the backpack he brought along and placed it near the amplifier.

"Why'd you bring the bug?"

"Just listen. I'm going to plug this into the amplifier, see," Frank declared, connecting the receiver to the amplifier with a jack. "Now listen real good," he commanded.

Jerry was still watching the young woman swaying back and forth as she leaned over the counter.

Frank took his brother's cherubic chin in his hand and jerked it toward him. Jerry was angelic with just a hint of the devil like his father. "Listen!"

Jerry gave him his *divided* attention.

"This jack is a priority jack. Once the receiver is turned on, whatever it picks up will override anything that goes into he amplifier from the stage."

"So?"

Frank knelt down next to the receiver and pointed to an on/off switch. "Don't turn this switch on until I get back."

"Where are you going?"

"Father Paul always has Confession at four on Saturdays."

"You going?"

"No. What are you nuts?"

"Then what?"

"To plant the microphone."

"Where?"

"In the confessional."

The younger brother finally forgot about Frenchy. "What! Bug the confessional! You can't do that! We'll get expelled, excommunicated. Or worse, they'll probably cut our balls off!"

"Don't worry about it. They're gonna need proof, and I'll get rid of it before they know what happened."

"They never needed proof before. I mean; it's not like they follow any laws or anything."

"What are you, a pussy?"

"No, but this is just crazy!"

"Look, I'm doing it, with or without you. Just make sure you don't flick on the switch until I get back, okay?"

"No way am I touching it." Jerry got distracted again watching the young woman's swaying hips.

Frank looked at his watch. *'Damn! Quarter to four. I've gotta' hurry.'*

He ran past the rectory to the church and entered the confessional. Fortunately, no one was yet on line, and Frank was not seen.

The confessional booth was dimly lit. Against the outer wall was a heavy curtain used to make the unheated booth more comfortable in winter. He looked at the metal grating between the box, the cubicle for the priest, and where the repentant sinner knelt. Most of it was in darkness. Taking the tiny microphone out of his pocket, Frank hooked it on to the metal grating. Suddenly, the door to the priest's box opened and Father Paul entered. Caught off guard, Frank panicked and slipped behind the curtain.

'Damn! If he catches me in here now, I'm really done for.'

The first sinner began the ritual with, "Bless me, Father, for I have sinned."

She was an elderly woman with a quivering, halting voice. To Frank, it seemed like it took her forever to spit out her sins of the soul. She was guilty of swearing, lying, smoking, drinking and a dozen others.

'Not very original.'

The priest didn't say anything until the woman had finished. Then he mumbled, "Your sins are forgiven you. For your penance say five Hail Marys and five Our Fathers."

'Pretty lenient. If that was me, he probably would've given me five weeks detention.'

Some dust from the curtain tickled his nose. Trying not to sneeze, he very cautiously moved his hand to scratch the itch, being careful not to ripple the curtain.

The next sinner told of how she was unfaithful to her husband on several occasions.

Again the priest was silent until the end, then remarked, "Your sins are forgiven you. For your penance say five Hail Marys and five Our Fathers."

'You've gotta be kidding me!' Frank was furious. *'This lady's screwin' everybody in town, except her husband, and she gets five Hail Marys and five Our Fathers. Is he listening? Maybe Father needs Mother Veronica's hearing aid. Maybe he's not even in there, and Father's just left a recording."*

Ten more sinners came and went after relieving their burden. Father Paul gave them all "five Hail Marys and five Our Fathers." It seemed to Frank the priest wasn't taking his duty seriously. If he wasn't, who would? If every sin was "five Hail Marys and five Our Fathers" worth of penance, then why shouldn't everyone go out and party?

While the sinners were confessing their sins, Congressman Ned Kane slipped into the church and knelt down in one of the pews. He waited for the last person to leave the confessional before standing and entering himself.

Mother Veronica was standing in the shadows of the stage outside the kissing booth. She watched carefully as some of the same boys kept returning to Frenchy. The good sister didn't fail to notice with each return, the kisses seemed to be getting longer. When the young woman leaned over the counter and revealed her cleavage, Mother Veronica was compelled to act.

"That's enough, young lady," she rasped, emerging from her unobserved vantage point. Devils and demons danced in her eyes. "I can see our little talk the other day didn't get through to you. You'd better give those hot lips of yours a rest."

Frenchy couldn't help but think the nuns were *everywhere* and knew *everything*. That was the only way they were even remotely close to God.

"But Mother, I'm raising so much cash for the church," she replied, lifting the nearly full moneybox from beneath the counter.

"The wages of sin!"

Jerry was watching from behind the booth. He nearly forgot about his brother's tardy return because of his preoccupation with Frenchy's gyrations.

"Take a break, young lady," the nun ordered. "I'll watch the money."

'You sure won't get any kisses,' Frenchy thought, as she exited through the rear of the booth. Seeing Jerry trying to avert his eyes, Frenchy smiled knowingly, and he blushed. "Want to get something to eat?" she asked.

Jerry suddenly knew where the idea of heaven came from. It was written all over Frenchy's face, her breasts and thighs. He was about to reply "Sure," but then remembered Frank. Simultaneously, Jerry understood what hell was. "I . . . can't. I've got to wait here for my brother."

"We'll only be gone a minute, unless of course . . . ."and then she giggled seductively.

He didn't give Frank a second thought. Taking Frenchy's hand, the two went for some pizza, but Jerry was thinking more of the dessert.

"Bless me father for I have sinned," the Congressman whispered to the priest. "It has been one week since my last confession and these are my sins."

There was a short pause; then he confessed slowly and clearly, "I stole money from my campaign funds and used it for bribes and, I'm sorry to say, to take my secretary on a cruise to the Caribbean. I lied a couple of times to the press about my views on Vietnam and the War on Poverty. Nothing real big, just little lies."

"Congressman Kane," the priest, recognizing the politician's voice as well his sins, replied, "we talked about this before. You really should stop doing these things."

Frank took shallow breaths hoping neither heard him. His nose began to run from the dust on the curtain. It was time to make a pact with the Almighty. *'God, I'll never do anything like this again. Just don't let me sneeze.'*

"I know I should, but there really is no other way to get elected. Besides, I can't really tell the people the truth. They're like children and would never understand it."

"And the woman?"

"Well, a public servant's due some happiness. My wife hasn't given me much in such a long time."

The dirt tickled Frank's nostrils again. He pinched them with his fingers.

"Maybe the two of you should come in and see me."

"The bitch – pardon my French, Father – will never do it. She's so busy with her women's groups and charities. You'd think she was a regular saint or something."

"Well, you should do your normal penance," the priest announced. *'Oh, don't tell me.'*

"Five Hail Marys and five Our Fathers?" the Congressman asked. *'Damn! I knew it!'*

"Yes. And try to mend your ways."

"I will, Father. Thanks."

Ned Kane left the confessional, and so did the priest.

Taking his first normal breath in what seemed like hours, Frank came out from behind the curtain and sneezed. He removed the microphone from off the grating. *'Damn! I would have given anything to have that confession broadcast. But, no one will ever believe me if I squeal, especially with my rep.'*

As he left the church, Frank stopped to let his eyes readjust to the bright light of day. Blinded temporarily, he couldn't believe what awaited him. There on the steps were scores of angry, silent people from the bazaar led by Mrs. Dorothy Kane, the Congressman's wife. Ever so slowly they were making a circle around Ned Kane who stood in their midst, the look of a caged animal on his face.

"I can explain," he urged, ever the politician. He seemed to shrivel in importance before Frank's eyes. No one was listening to Ned Kane. They wouldn't ever again. He was lucky there were two policemen on the grounds or else the crowd would have killed him right there.

After the Congressman was removed, Jerry came running up the steps holding on to Frenchy's hand, "Boy, you really got him."

"What do you mean?" a bewildered Frank asked. "What's happening?"

"Oh, I see. Mum's the word," the brother answered, winking. "It's all right. You can talk. She's with me now."

"Jerry, I don't know what the hell you're talking about."

"The confession. We heard the whole thing over the speakers. Everybody did. I figured you must have put the switch on."

"I didn't touch it. I was stuck in the confessional the whole time."

"Well, then, who put the switch on?"

It is said God works in mysterious ways and chooses even stranger instruments. When the rock band began its first song, the speakers went dead. Even the hard-of-hearing Mother Veronica knew something was wrong. Busy meddling in other peoples' business, she watched as the stage manager walked past the kissing booth on his way to inspect the amplifier behind the stage. Momentarily leaving her post, the nun followed him.

"What's the matter?" she asked.

The manager, without turning around to see he was speaking to a nun, replied, "It's a bitch."

Mother Veronica, bending over inspecting Frank's wireless receiver, thought the manager remarked, *It's the switch*. Noticing it was off, she flipped the switch on. To Mother Veronica, the conversation over the speaker was garbled, but at least she knew something was coming over it. She looked proudly at him and declared, "It's fixed. All it took was a little help from God."

The manager, turned around abruptly, saying, "What the fu . . ." but stopped short when he saw the nun. Flustered, he continued, "I'm sorry, sister."

"You can go back to your stage now, young man," she noted breathlessly, as she observed his open shirt and hairy chest. "I've taken care of the problem."

Afterwards, no one in his right mind had a satisfactory answer for what had happened. Certainly not the brothers. But, Mother Veronica did. She called it a "miracle."

That's when the pilgrims began making St. Rose a regular stop on their holy rounds. After all, how many modern supernatural events have there been? Money came pouring in from the sale of post cards, stationary, and figurines. The number-one item was an amulet of tiny speakers the faithful could dangle around their necks.

The church and school were saved. Father Paul, literally convinced that the Supreme Being intervened, couldn't have been happier. The Congressman, disgraced and loathed, confessed his crimes and was kicked out of office. Mother Veronica, still always certain and frequently wrong, remained as the principal of the high school.

Jerry actually fell in love with Frenchy and eventually spent most of his time with her.

Frank laughed whenever anyone mentioned "the miracle of St. Rose." Yet, there was doubt in his mind. Every now and again he found himself saying, "Who knows, maybe it was."

Biography of
Constance M. Schmidt

Constance Schmidt was born and raised in Rio Rancho, New Mexico. She and her husband Bill spent ten years in Saudi Arabia, an experience that provided her with a treasure of stories about life in that exotic place, as well as traveling through other neighboring third world countries where coping with 'surprises' and often danger became part of the Schmidt's life experiences.

Connie's story about a stalker caught our attention. The group thought you'd be interested to read this true story.

THE STALKER

Non-fiction

by Constance M. Schmidt

How well do you know your neighbors; the couple next door; the family who lives at the end of the block; what about the man and woman who live across the street; or that amiable man who cleans carpets and whose wife just had a baby? They live several blocks away; or that nice looking man who lives across town and who coaches the girl's basketball team? Even though these people are separated by buildings and miles, some living in big houses; some in small; some have children; some don't; some are married; some single. No matter what the situation, they are all neighbors.

How can you tell exactly what kind of neighbor it is? You probably will never know. Let me tell you my story.

One morning at approximately 7:30 a.m. on my way to play golf, I pulled out of my driveway and noticed a red car at the end of my street in front of a neighbor's house. Sensing he was a stranger, I pulled up next to his car and asked if there was a problem . . . all the time noticing he was a nice looking young man.

Imagine my shock when he said, "I am looking for Constance Schmidt."

At 7:30 a.m. I am neither awake nor bright, so with a groggy mind, my reply was, "I am Constance Schmidt."

He then proceeded to tell me I was supposed to have a massage that morning. In my total ignorance, I then said, "Oh! There must be some mistake," and I took off for the golf course. Would you believe I forgot about the whole incident?

Several evenings later as I was getting grocery bags out of the trunk of my car, I observed a red car go by very very slowly. Thinking it was my next-door neighbor who also had a red car, I waved, and then after taking a second look, I realized the man was much younger than my neighbor. Next thing I know the red car, having reached the end of my street had turned around and was about to pass my house again. Finally, my antenna went up. I ran out of the garage and tried to see his license plate. All I could tell in the dusk of evening was that the plate was from out-of-state.

I screamed, "You're sick," then quickly ran inside and called the police. Well, even though an officer took down all the information, I learned later there was no follow up. In frustration I notified all the neighbors in my complex about what had happened and to keep an eye out for this red car with an out-of-state license plate. Several people saw the car driving around the complex occasionally, but they also could not get his plate number.

One and a half weeks later, as I was turning into my street, I noticed the red car parked in front of a neighbor's house – and no one was in it. I was very frightened not knowing where he might be hiding. Could he have broken into my home? Cautiously I entered my home and thank goodness, he was not there. I phoned my neighbor where the red car was parked. My neighbor told me that when he saw this red car, he went outside and approached the man, who at this point had started walking down the path that lies behind my house. My neighbor assured the stranger that the person he was looking for did not live in this neighborhood. At the same time, my neighbor made a mental note of the car's license plate number.

At last, with this information in hand, I called a detective who worked with our local police force and told him the whole story. Several days later, he stopped by to tell me the man had been arrested on sexual charges in a mid-western state, but he was never indicted.

The detective refused to give me the man's name, but with the help of a close friend, I did manage to find out his name and where he lived. It seems he was married, had three children; lived in a nice large home at the end of town and worked as a nurse in a local nursing home.

Shortly after, I was surprised to read an article in the paper stating that this same individual was starting a carpet cleaning company. Can you envision this person coming into your home?

His company car was now a red van . . . neighbors behind my house saw the van parked in several different areas in our complex . . . sometimes empty. From time to time he would ask people where I lived.

By now I had become too frightened to go out in the evening. Finally, I convinced the detective to do something to protect me. After what seemed an eternity, he did bring some mug shots to show me. All the people looked the same . . . same color hair; same age. Unfortunately I could not identify a picture of the man who was devastating my life. Consequently the stalker was once again not indicted.

Thank heaven, eventually he stopped coming into my complex. I guess he zeroed in on other potential prey. The last I heard, he was coaching the girl's basketball team at a local school. This sick individual probably still lives in the same house, has the same neighbors, still cleans neighbor's houses, and still coaches the girls' team.

My stalker was part of a community . . . a neighbor.

How well do you really know your neighbors???

Biography of
Joann Wayne Sloan

Born in Miami, Florida, Joann Wayne Sloan lived all of her adult life in New York, New Jersey, Pennsylvania and Georgia. She earned her B.A. and M.A. at Rowan University (formerly Glassboro State College) in New Jersey and a Ph.D. at the University of Delaware. She taught both psychology and sociology in colleges in New Jersey and New York, and within The University System of Georgia, where she also served on the editorial board of a textbook publisher.

Writing became a part of her life when at age ten she created (by hand and in pencil!) a neighborhood newspaper. This was followed at age twelve by a travelogue of England (though she had never been in England!),and a short story written at age fifteen (earning her first rejection slip!). In New Jersey, she published a poem in *Sunshine* Magazine and an article and photograph on pewter in a collectors' magazine. In Georgia a selection of her photographs were published in a college literary journal and throughout her career various writings in her academic discipline have been published.

The Call of the Loon, her first attempt at a novel was inspired by the number of professional women who are choosing to combine family with downsized careers.

CALL OF THE LOON

Fiction

by Joann Sloan

PROLOGUE

The attack came without warning. She felt a hard tug on her handbag and then the sharp pain of a knife cutting into her arm. Wheeling around in shock, she stared into the face of her assailant. His eyes held hers for only a moment, but it seemed a lifetime. She screamed and struck out with the fist that held her keys, but he moved with rocket speed, grabbing her handbag and knocking her off balance with a ruthless punch to the ribs that sent her reeling to the sidewalk. As she hit the concrete, the sound of his footsteps running away echoed in her ear, but the agonizing pain in her chest made chase impossible.

Dazed, she struggled to her feet. Bleeding and hunched over in pain, she staggered the few remaining yards to her building. Inside her apartment, she bolted the door behind her, and leaned against it, gasping for breath. Blood ran down her arm and dripped onto the carpet. Still straining with each breath, she clutched her ribs with her good arm and stumbled to the kitchen. Wrapping a dishtowel clumsily around the gash, she dialed 911.

"I've been attacked. I'm bleeding," she caught her breath between words, as she murmured her name and address. The phone slipped out of her hand, the instrument dangling at the end of its cord, as she slid down the wall. She struggled to stay calm, until she heard sirens in the distance. Grimacing from the pain, she pulled herself up and limped to the door, but didn't unsnap the bolt until she heard the unmistakable sounds of the police on the other side.

Minutes later, the ambulance arrived and the attendants efficiently attended to her wound. "You're going to need a couple of stitches in that, Ma'am. They'll take care of it when we get you to the emergency room."

"I don't want to go to the emergency room," she said. "I'll go to my doctor in the morning." She felt violated and she would never feel safe here again. Now, she wished she hadn't called for help. She wished she'd bandaged the cut and gone to bed. She just wanted everyone to go away and leave her alone. Breath came easier now, but the pain was still intense.

"You can't do that, Ma'am. You need stitches to close that cut and we can't tell if any of your ribs are broken without x-rays. You have to let us take you to the emergency room."

"They're right," said one of the officers. "Do you have a relative or friend you can call to meet you there?"

"No. No one I can call at this hour." She knew they were right. Her injuries did require more medical attention than the paramedics could give them. "All right," she said. "I'll go." Strong arms gently lifted her onto the stretcher.

"Give us a minute, fellows," an officer said. "We need some information for our report."

She turned to the officers and answered their questions. Yes, he had her handbag. No, he hadn't attempted to rape her. No, she couldn't identify him if she saw him again. No, she hadn't seen anyone else around, who might be a witness. All she could remember were those frighteningly cold eyes. Turning her head into the stretcher, she finally gave way to tears.

CHAPTER 1

The packing was complete, Megan looked at the boxes lined up against the wall, taped, addressed, and numbered. "Waifs," she muttered to herself. "They look like waifs. frightened children wondering what will happen next."

"You're projecting," Hannah, the psychology professor back home at Franklin College would have said. "You're the one whose scared."

And, she'd probably be right. I am a little frightened, Megan thought, as she felt the butterflies fluttering around in her stomach.

Arriving in the city three years ago, she had needed to prove that she could be a successful attorney in the "big leagues" of the legal profession. She had accomplished that goal brilliantly after moving to Philadelphia from Riverside, her hometown on the banks of the St. Lawrence River in upstate New York. Now she was leaving it behind her. She pulled the strap of her new handbag over her shoulder, picked up her overnight case and resolutely shut the door behind her.

Last week, she had won a major case defending a popular entertainer from charges brought by his unscrupulous manager. She glowed from the hard fought victory, as she walked out onto the courthouse steps, only thirty-three years old, yet the ultimate professional in a beige wool suit and navy blue v-necked blouse, her brown Gucci bag hanging from her shoulder, matching briefcase in her other hand, and short dark curls framing her smiling face.

"How do you feel winning a big one like this, Ms. Kearney?"

"Do you really think your client is innocent, Megan?"

"How did you feel, when the jury was out for so long."

Cameras taped for the six o'clock news and print reporters hastily scribbled down her answers.

She had been made a junior partner and she was living her dream, but in spite of the glow, in spite of the thrill of winning, she was troubled. Instead of feeling light-hearted and fulfilled, she had been experiencing her own private tug-of-war.

Excited, as she always was, by the adrenaline rush that exhilarated her when a jury filed in to announce its verdict, there was also the frustration of twelve and fourteen-hour days standing in the way of a personal life. She wanted to fall in love, marry, and have children, a goal continuously thwarted by her hectic schedule.

Her ambition to be the best, to enter politics and establish herself as a doer, fought with her desire to be near her family and to have a family of her own. The longer she stayed in the city, the closer she came to realizing the former, but the farther she was from the latter.

She scarcely had time for a social life. How would she have time for a family?

Now, as her silver Acura slipped in and out of the heavy Broad Street traffic, she griped the steering wheel, aware of the tension across her shoulders. She swung onto the Northern Extension of the Pennsylvania Turnpike and, when buildings and factories began to give way to tracts of houses, she felt her body begin to relax. Soon, the graceful Pocono Mountains, a dozen shades of early summer green, seemed to wrap themselves around her.

As the miles sped by, her thoughts turned to home and to her friends. She laughed thinking of Charlie and Jean. According to Jean, her college roommate and her buddy since grammar school, Charlie was turning cartwheels at the prospect of having Megan return to work in his law firm. He had hired her right out of law school and claimed she was irreplaceable. After her parents, he was the first one she had called to say she was coming home.

When it was settled that she would return to her old job, she said, "Please tell me that the Evans place is still on the market."

"Sure is. Jack Mc Cord and I were just talking about it this weekend. He figures that now that summer is here, someone will snap it up."

"Will you call him right away for me, Charlie and ask him to put a bid in for me. It's exactly the house I want."

Everything is going perfectly, she thought. As the car crossed the New York State line the tires sang along with her; home, I'm going home. The senior partners had insisted that she take a leave of absence rather than resign, but she knew she had made the right decision. Her future was in Riverside.

In the distance, she saw a small plane revving its motor at the end of an air strip beside the highway. She thought of Eric. Eric Waterman, the handsome professor of history at Franklin College, Riverside's major claim to fame. They had dated before she left, but Eric had been elusive. It would seem that everything was going well between them and she was sure that he felt as drawn to her, as she to him. But then, he always pulled back, leaving her doubting her natural instincts.

Watching the plane taxi down the runway reminded her of a plane ride she had taken over the Thousand Islands with Eric. It had been awesome seeing the familiar landscape from the air, but his arm holding her tightly made the flight even more exciting and pleasurable.

The June air was hot, but inside the car with the air conditioner turned on, Megan was comfortable. The blue Bermuda shorts and red-stripped tee shirt had been the right choice. The car moved effortlessly through the New York landscape. She turned on the radio and sang along with Frank Sinatra, ". . . icy fingers run up and down my spine." Eric . . . They had danced to that song at the River House one Saturday night. ". . . that old black magic has me in its spell." He had held her tightly against him, her head resting on his shoulder. When the music ended, Eric had loosened his hold and had looked into her eyes for a moment before they walked back to their table. It had been a magic moment, but it quickly vanished. At her door, he had kissed her, as he always did, but with his usual friendly kiss. His touch had made her tremble and she had been sure that he felt something, too; but, if he had, he had kept it to himself.

She wondered, as she had many times over these last three years, just how much Eric's attitude had to do with her leaving home. Her mother and father, Sarah and Brian, had taught at Franklin college for years and, when Eric joined the faculty, Sara had brought him home to dinner. Megan had taken one look and thought, wow! Tall and stunningly handsome in a Nordic kind of way, he had thick blond hair, amazing blue eyes, and an appealing dimple in his chin. His looks fulfilled all her girlish fantasies, but he was distant from the beginning. He had asked her out from time to time, but weeks had gone by between his calls.

She had been so enthralled with him that for a while, she had turned down other dates, preferring to wait for his call. When it had become evident that he wasn't going to let the relationship become serious, she had begun to see other men. But none of them stirred up her emotions the way Eric did. Her heart beat faster every time she recognized his sensuous voice on the phone.

"What is it with Eric?" Megan had asked her mother. "You see him every day at the college. What's he like there?"

"Like any other professor . . . busy with his classes," Sarah said. "Why do you ask?"

"When we're together, I'm sure he's feeling something for me, but then he pulls back."

"I don't know, honey. Rumor around the campus has it that his marriage back in Massachusetts was volatile and the divorce was messy. He's probably still numb. With a little effort, I'm sure you can coax him out of his shell."

Megan had done plenty of 'coaxing' with Eric, but nothing had come of it. The memory of his coolness still puzzled and frustrated her. Maybe things would be different, when she returned home.

She was hungry when she sped into Syracuse, but she didn't want to stop. Her mother would have a meal prepared for her. She could wait. She maneuvered through the heavy city traffic, passing the University exit and the huge Carousel Mall. Everything was so familiar. It was like being back among old friends. The traffic began to thin and soon she recognized the tip of Oneida Lake. Excitement began to build within her. It wouldn't be long now.

She turned off Route 81, just before the road swooped up onto the International Bridge. A shiver of anticipation shot up her spine. She could almost, but not quite, see the river. She was sure she could smell it and in a few miles, there it was, stretched out beside the road and daring her not to stop. She pulled onto a viewing plaza, turned off the motor, and got out of the car. In the twilight, the St. Lawrence River lay before her in all its magnificence. Megan walked over to a stone fence and breathed deeply. She was home. Here was the river . . . her river.

The islands looked as if they had been tossed like stones, landing haphazardly in the water. They were all sizes, but the tiny ones intrigued her the most. One was barely big enough for the house that stood in the middle of it and another was only a dozen or so feet across. On a third, a rowboat lay on its side, its oars leaning against the wall of a bright red cottage. Her stomach doing flip-flops, she returned to the car for the last few miles of her journey home.

Biography of
Trudie Peterson

Trudie Nehse Peterson has written a compelling story about growing up during the great depression of the 30's. This work is part of her life's biography, a book she is composing as a memoir. She was born on a houseboat in Memphis, as the story tells us, but she has lived in New York and Ocean Pines, Maryland, for long periods of time. Trudie and her husband Joe have two children. Now living in The Villages where she enjoys writing, Trudie also has been involved in other creative arts. She paints and has played in numerous theatrical productions while living in Maryland

MY BOX OF THINGS

a memoir

by Trudie Peterson

I was born on the Mississippi river. That's what they wrote on my birth certificate – January 1926.

Born at the foot of Jefferson Street in Memphis, Tennessee. I lived on our boat at my father's boatyard. His name was Frank Nehse from Hamburg Germany, and as old as my granddad. His bride, Alice my mother, was literally a child-bride and he was anxious to have a son. When I was due to make an appearance in the world, Mother hired a midwife and my father had to settle for a girl – me.

I remember little of those days as I was a toddler, but we spoke only German. Now it seems strange to me that it took many years to transfer our words and thoughts into English.

Mother decorated the house boat's wrap-around porch with flower pots, she hung pretty curtains inside plus installing a rope railing to prevent little ones from falling into the water below.

Living on a boat was hard. Dishes had to be secured from tumbling and breaking. Health hazzards lurked everywhere. For instance one night a rat crawled onto my crib and bit my toe. Mother wakened and screamed as he ran across her bed. She hated living on that river boat.

When I was less than two years old, a boat named Trudie slipped it's mooring in a storm. Father, along with several helpers, set out to rescue it. His left arm got caught in the motor and had to be amputated.

Mother told me later that he'd been drinking. Pretty soon after that, we moved to a house.

I can remember every day running up a path to greet my dad when he returned home evenings. Now on shore, having him hold me I would feel the stub of his arm. He taught me German songs and drilled me on proper German language. I clearly remember his group of friends who often came to our house, congregating in the back room behind a curtain-covered doorway. They laughed, drank and smoked ignoring my mother's anger.

Their marriage had been failing for a long time. I was two years old when my brother Frank was born. Now my father had his little boy, a fleeting thing, for no sooner had he been born than mother, in great distress, put both of us in a baby carriage and left.

I was sent to board with a couple named Katie and Myrick who had two daughters; Wilma and Katherine. I was the youngest in the household and enjoyed lots of attention. A friendly old goat pulled me around the yard in a cart.

Myrick, the man of the house, kept chickens. I helped feed them, pick up fresh eggs, and place fake eggs under the hens. He worked at the poorhouse in the day time, at night he'd chew and spit the juice at Katie's pots. Often times he'd miss, making Katie very angry.

When baby chicks hatched, they were brought into the kitchen near the pot-bellied stove. It delighted me to touch them and hear the peeping.

I learned that my brother Frank was living on a farm not too distant, but I never got to see him. Occasionally Father came to visit me, but he had arguments over my clothing. I guess Father still thought I should have been a boy. Mother accepted my being a girl, but on father's visits, my keepers dressed me according to my father's demands. Mother also visited me often.

Living in this house with Katie and her family was really a *Rebecca of Sunnybrook Farm* fantasy. It was the best time of my life – but changes were in the air.

Mother was disturbed that I was so becoming so attached to this family, She had no choice but to place me in an orphanage named Saint

Mary's where I never left the building except family visits and once a year riding to summer camp in Little Rock, Arkansas.

The orphanage was a majestic building with long halls and mahogany walls.

The third floor held the two school rooms. They were decorated with saints, strings of wooden prayer beads and wall carvings. The elegant hardwood floors were kept meticulously waxed. We had to wax them on our hands and knees with wax that looked like a bar of soap. We'd rub the wax on, then polish it off. Seemed like there were miles and miles of floor we had to scrub and wax.

The Sisters of the Poor from Boston were in charge. I received my schooling, religious training, room and board in this very austere building. Each morning at six o'clock we sprang up from bed to stand, to recite the Angelus. Then we washed and dressed for the day's activities and religious training. I was young, so my baths were in a tin tub by colored servants whom I loved. This was the only time during my confinement in the orphanage that I experienced affection and touching.

We went to chapel every morning where there was a box of white starched chapel hats. We put them on when entering and placed them back into the box when we left. The church was dark and dingy, a very scarey place for me. I believed the statues of the saints were actually alive, dealing out retribution or rewards and would punish me if I did something wrong. These statues succeeded in putting the fear of God into me, especially when the nuns reinforced my fear by telling stories about saints that terrified me. I doubt that it was their ambition to frighten little kids, but they sure scared me.

Halloween parties were held in a room with windows on three sides. In the middle of a spooky story, some of the sisters would run outside and act up in front of the window, making us believe they were ghosts of some kind. Talk about being scared., yes we were.

Feelings of fear and loneliness came over me every day. I prayed and prayed, not daring to leave any thought or wish unsaid. My recurring dream of mother dead was very unsettling. I worried that she'd never get me out. We attended group prayers six or seven times a day, plus Bible readings. By the time I reached ten, I was pretty much prayed out.

When Mother came to visit in the orphanage dining room, my brother Frank was allowed to join us. Otherwise he was lost to me. Yet sometimes I saw him playing in another section of the yard with other boys. I always loudly proclaimed to my friends, "There's Frank, he's my brother."

Sundays if Mother happened to bring a candy bar or cookies, the cookies were given to a nun who promptly divided each into sixteen pieces (imagine dividing a five-cent Hershey chocolate bar into sixteen pieces?)

Mother was a selfish person in keeping us from most family help. Grandparents Mama and Granddaddy were our only family. They could visit us with mother's permission.

As we walked in the school halls it was important to keep in line. We were never hugged or given praise for anything, only scolding or correcting. School was on the third floor. Two rooms. One for children up to grade eight, the other for high school. I remember doing well in my studies and tried to rush ahead to higher grades. Forth grade you had an ink well.

We were required to memorize poems. The two I recall were *The Gingham Dog and the Calico Cat* and *Little Orphan Annie*. I enjoyed moving to the next row, each class in a row, and dreamed of the day I would reach the next room of high school.

We were allowed no singing other than hymns or gospel songs and *The Battle Hymn of the Republic*. How powerful those words.

"Mine eyes have seen the power of the coming of the Lord."

I believed I had actually seen the Lord. Another song that is burned into my memory,

"Jesus loves me, this I know, because the Bible tells me so,

Little ones to him belong, They are weak, but he is strong."

Oh yes, these words he spoke to me personally, I was certain that Jesus loved me and I was a little one.

Radios or movies didn't exist during our stay at the orphanage. Card playing was also taboo. When we were taken outside by Mother (once a month) we were forbidden to travel in buses, or eat in restaurants. Fortunately Mother had enough sense to break the rules, thank goodness. In truth, the few times we were out, I was in awe to view people going about their business. Street sounds were fascinating, and Mother sang a song, *Five foot two, eyes of blue, oh how she could kutchi koo, has anybody seen my gal?* a song that would never have come from the nun's lips.

Once I visited Mama (my grandma) and she took me to a local beauty contest in town. Some one bought me a bathing suit and entered me in the contest. I came in second and a picture was taken to celebrate the occasion. I was thrilled at the honor, but couldn't help wondering what would have happened if I'd won first place and made the local papers. Oh my!

When I visited Mama (my grandmother), my mother never took me to her place, I loved a feather mattress in her bedroom. When I lay in it, I disappeared from view. Sometimes at suppertime Mama (grandma) would place a plate of food on the back step. Intrigued, I would watch for a person to appear. They would stand out by the bushes and the plate would vanish, but later be returned empty. I asked why the person stayed outside. Mama said it was pride.

It was poverty.

All food at the orphanage had to be eaten. If I left a part of a potato uneaten on my lunch plate, it would appear again at supper time. I learned at a young age to hold my breath to swallow things, like cream onions I didn't like.

When I was school age, I got to leave The Home for Poor Children. Mother got married again. We moved into a home together as a family. This was Mother's first home since leaving Father. Sadly the marriage was not likely to last. Paydays were always a problem. My new father brought home groceries, but no money and always with liquor on his breath. There were many arguments and even at my young age, I could see the handwriting on the wall. Yet there were good times, too.

I remember Christmas when all my toys had mysteriously disappeared, my favorites were a wicker baby carriage and a settee and chair. On Christmas morning they appeared under the tree freshly painted. I was happy and delighted.

During this time, I got to visit my grand parents a lot. Mama (grandma) and Granddaddy, who was a Memphis policeman, and the family owned and ran a grocery store and butcher shop. They also raised chickens and terrier puppies that I could play with, and kept a vegetable garden I could pick from. They had three daughters, but Alice the oldest, was the only one to give them grandchildren. Aunt Bobbie (Lavarah) lived at home, and Aunt Mamie (Mary Lee) had gone to California.

One day our family was out walking when Frank, tripped over a sewer grate and lost a shoe. This caused a lot of dismay and argument. When we got home Frank was very sick running a high fever. He ended up in the hospital with scarlet fever, a dangerous illness, that was common in those days. I was allowed to visit him, but only behind a glass wall, as the disease was highly contagious. I brought him many of my things including favorite books and toys, newly acquired which ended up being burned when he left the hospital.

On my birthday, one year Mother baked me a cake with white icing and coconut on top. I thought the coconut looked like cut-up strings to me and I began to cry, but mother explained that the coconut was something special and decorative and, of course, I ate it with pleasure. That was the only birthday cake I'd ever had.

Mother's marriage was over before it began. Drinking problems are hard to deal with and memories of drunk men remain burned in my memory. Both of my dads drank to excess, but in the case of husband number three, he had the misfortune while he was sleeping off a drunk episode, to call out the name, "Lois." Mother, whose name was Alice, scribbled the name *Lois* with Mercurochrome on his chest and packed us up again to leave.

So back to The Home for Poor Children we went. This time with my brother Frank I became sad and frustrated because I never got to talk to him. No one was allowed to speak as we passed each other in the halls, but we did reach out and touch hands.

The day we returned to the home, the girls gathered around me complimenting my nice new clothes; a pretty print dress with matching panties (made from flour sacks). Frank had a matching tie. Sadly for us, the following week our new clothing was thrown into a size bin, to be worn by anyone that size. I felt anger. It was directed to mother for leaving us here. All my things were gone. It seemed to me that the sisters went to great trouble to make sure I never got to wear my special things again.

Mother had also brought our toys from home and they were put in the toy room. We no longer owned them, but shared them. There was no room for personal belongings – they were shared.

As I look back now on my life in the orphanage, I clearly see that my individuality was sheared off in little ways each day. I had to struggle to keep important aspects of my personality for my very own. Often when I cried when another girl wore one of my dresses, I was quickly and strongly scolded for my selfishness. But who would enjoy sharing everything you once owned with sixteen girls? No speaking was allowed until three in the afternoon when school and the Bible readings were over. Complaints fell on deaf ears.

In this silent and frustrating atmosphere, I grew close to God. He was my only friend and no one could hear our conversations. Somehow, I gained new confidence and self assuredness, I began to assert myself out loud, but the sisters would have none of it.

Sometimes they would sneak up on us. They wore spongy-soled shoes and walked in silence, but they could not subdue the tell-tale tinkle of prayer beads and a cross that dangled at their waists. Still they were cagey, if a nun was on a spying mission, she held her rope of beads still, descending on her prey in silence.

If a girl in our room got out of bed at night, our caregivers laid a trap of talcum on the floor, a sure strategy to detect foot prints. The girls tried to overcome this obstacle by walking on the molding, but that never worked. So, if a girl had to go to the bathroom, the talcum powder was indisputable evidence.

The orphanage preferred group punishment, so we all had to pay a price for a long list of minor offences. The punishment was often confinement to our rooms with only bread and water, stale or moldy bread, I might add. We were never given an explanation of the rules, nor did we have the courage to question the sister's right to punish us.

Amazingly we survived.

When Frank was seven years old, he and two other boys escaped from the home. I was terrified. The orphanage was surrounded by a high iron fence and its own guard dog Don O Blitzen. I felt certain I'd never again see my little brother. Thank God, the boys were discovered fishing in the Mississippi river. I never learned the punishment they received.

We believed all the nuns were bald under their head gear and we plotted to bump into one, hoping the head-piece would fall off and reveal a shiny dome. We tried in many small ways to make this happen, but we never succeeded. In our quest to see a naked head, sometimes we stood on our beds to peek through a tiny window into sister's room. Alas, we only caught her at prayer, and wondered if her prayers were dedicated to the little sinners in our room.

Mother went to great pains to warn me never to mention the fact that I had a live father. Only *single* mothers or fathers were permitted to enroll children there and many of the youngsters *did* have one parent. I forgot these instructions one day when a man came to the fence and called my name, "Trudie." I walked to the fence to see what the stranger wanted. He gave me a bag of candy and then left. When I told Mother, she became upset, certain that the stranger was my dad wanting to get a glimpse of his daughter. She was afraid the sisters would find out that there was a father in our family, and Frank and I would be kicked out of the orphanage. (This was a real worry).

Times were very hard for Mother. She worked at the Telegraph Postal Union so did her sister, Mamie, but they worked only on weekends and holidays and when someone else was absent. Her income was not enough to support a family, even though she tried to supplement it by crocheting samples for the Woolworth Company. Occasionally, she got work playing the organ at the church. (The depression was a disaster for everyone.)

Memphis had a Cotton Parade and I had dreamed for years of being the Queen, but had to settle for appearing as a bird. In my finery, new shoes and wearing a colorful bird costume, I marched miles and miles, and got large blisters on my feet. Still in pain, the newspaper did photograph me in my grand costume and it appeared the following day. Fortunately the nuns didn't notice it or bother to read that part of the paper and I escaped punishment.

When I was six and Frank four, after three years here, our mother left us alone at the home to seek her fortune in New York. I was full of hope because she had promised to come soon and take both of us out of the orphanage.

Now, as I look back, I believe her motivation came from a dramatic and tragic incident in our family: the death of her father.

Granddaddy Jack was a large man, not tall, but so big that it was almost impossible to sit on his lap. Grandmother was so slim that Granddaddy teasingly called her "Mary Bones." Mother sometimes depended on her parents for help which they gave willingly. Who knows what they thought of her two failed marriages and two children to support.

The day Granddaddy was murdered he wasn't feeling well. He had what he referred to as the "heebie geebies," but he knew, or felt, something was wrong and went to the phone in the back of the store to call his doctor. As he described his illness to the physician, a black man entered the store and asked to use the phone. Grandmother was working that day in the store and said,.

"Sure, but wait until my husband finishes his call,"

When Grandfather hung up the phone, and stepped back into the store, the man pulled out a pistol and shot him. He fell dead at Mama's (Grand mother's) feet.

1931 was a tough year for the entire family. In despair, Mother made plans to leave us behind and move to New York and to eventually to bring Frank and me to live with her. She took five years in New York making plans. She had to move from her furnished room to a small apartment. Frank and I waited excitedly and with great hope, for the 'magic day.' I had all the post cards she sent of the Statue of Liberty, The Empire State Building and snow scenes. I dreamed of the day.

June of 1936, the last week at the orphanage I was due to perform in a piano recital and mother was asked to supply a white dress for me. Ever resourceful, she crocheted an artistic original

When the nuns inspected the charming frock, they were horrified at the many holes and open spaces. The dress was beautiful but not suitable they announced. The sister's got rid of it, much to my distress. I had to wear a substitute and I was angry. What was it about Mother, that never seemed to go right?

Finally Grandmother came to remove us from the home and put us on a Greyhound bus for the three day trip to New York and mother. Grandma gave each of us a big hug and a kiss. Then she handed me a small bag of things, handkerchief, underwear, my cards, and not much else.

"Bye, Grandma, I'll miss you," I cried as she pinned money to my undershirt.

"You take care of Frank, and give your mother a kiss for me, she answered and dabbed her eyes a little.

The bus pulled away and I had something like three dollars I was frightened to spend, a normal reaction for someone who had never been exposed to people in public places or ever having any cash. We learned to sleep sitting up in our seats and got our meals at bus stops.

At the orphanage food always arrived at our table from the basement dumbwaiter and we ate whatever there was without comment. Now we got exposed to new and glorious treats, like tomato juice, and there was money to buy them. I quickly forgot my fright about spending.

At each bus stop, there remained one last annoyance from the orphanage. A social worker appeared to insure our safety. Frank took this as a challenge, perhaps fearing that we'd be forced back to the home.

At our last stop he disappeared, hiding in the men's room. I cried outside the door, begging him to come out and got help from the other passengers. However, one time he escaped through an open window and I panicked that he was gone forever. But when the bus left, he appeared in the seat next to me and all was well as we arrived in New York.

The bus finally reached Pennsylvania Station where Mother worked. We quickly found her and enjoyed minutes of hugs and kisses. Then came one last instruction from the orphanage. "Mother, we have to find the social worker assigned by the home and tell her about our safe arrival."

"But of course," laughed Mother. She grabbed each of us beside her as we went to find the woman. We were ready for a new beginning.

Biography of
Mary Lois Sanders

Mary Lois Sanders is a professional writer and editor and an expert on American Indian traditions, history and customs. Raised in the south, she received a BA and a MA in music from Baylor University in Texas. Mary Lois has maintained her interest in music and in addition is very interested in theater arts and Opera. She is presently working on a young adult novel, *Vision Seeker*, about a fascinating young Indian, Running Girl, who becomes a prophet for her tribe.

THE DUEL

Fiction

by Mary Lois Sanders

The Champion was big, mean and two fisted. Wherever he walked guys scattered to let him pass. He was Gorgeous Gordon, every female's dream, the state Heavy-weight Wrestling Champ, the toughest tackle on the football team, the ultimate best ice cream eater Haddleyville High had ever known.

The Challenger was scrawny, painfully polite and two left footed. Guys jostled him when they passed. No females dreamed of him. He was Freckles Fremont, computer whiz, poster boy for the near sighted, a nerd's nerd and he had a secret weapon.

The Challenge was made in May on the next-to-the-next-to-the-last day of school. Freckles Fremont approached Gorgeous Gordon in his lair, the sport jock tables at the front of the cafeteria. He hesitated only a moment before suddenly throwing a stack of paper napkins onto GG's plate. A collective gasp surged through the surrounding crowd. No one got between the Champ and his lunch!

Slowly, GG pushed back his chair, rose to his considerable height and glared down at Freckles. The Champ held up one napkin only but the familiar logo and colors of the Ice Cream Emporium could be seen by all.

"I challenge you, Gordon, to an ice cream duel," Freckles shouted in his high-pitched tenor voice. "Name your Seconds!"

Unthinkable! The Champion had been challenged. The gauntlet thrown down. The proverbial slap of insult dealt. Reputations would be won and lost on the dip of a spoon!

Freckles chose as his Seconds Garland Hoffmeyer, Chess Club President, and Brigitte d'Amboise, founder and guiding light of the French Haitian Student Organization.

Gorgeous Gordon chose as his Seconds Soccer Team Captain, Ahmed Faraz, and Gwynn Bostwick, Golf Team Captain, State Women's Amateur Golf Champ and girlfriend.

These worthies readied all necessary equipment. Favorite spoons were polished, spares acquired; towels and buckets were assembled; the Referee appointed.

Champion and Challenger spent last hours preparing. GG pumped his normal 2 hours of iron each day, ate his regular enormous meals and belched with alacrity. Freckles practiced his new gulping technique based on the theory that ice cream was merely thick liquid and could therefore be tolerated in great quantities.

Then on the day, immediately after the last bell of the school year, the principals assembled at the appointed spot.

The gathered crowd murmured in hushed tones. Local TV news teams waited for the duel to begin. Suddenly, from each end of the Mall, the duelists appeared.

Gorgeous Gordon was gorgeous, as usual. He strutted toward the Ice Cream Emporium with pride. He wore black wrestling togs and a swirling black satin cape, "GG" emblazoned on the back. His shoulder-length black hair bounced with each step. His bulging muscles glistened. He was magnificent. A woman in the crowd swooned.

Freckles Fremont was Freckles Fremont. Unassuming, polished and pressed within an inch of his life, bow tie straight, collar buttoned down. He stumbled only once as he reached the Emporium's doorway. No one swooned. However, those looking closely saw an unusually bright gleam in his eyes. He was determined. He was ready. He was a bottomless pit waiting to be filled!

The duelists took their seats at the table in the center of the Emporium. The Referee, Mort, The Snort, Watkins, called everyone to attention.

"Hear ye, hear ye! All who are gathered to witness this duel give heed to my voice! Now hear the rules by which this duel shall proceed. Each duelist will consume, completely, one scoop each of the 26 flavors featured by the Emporium."

A murmur ran through the crowd. 26 scoops! The Snort, holding up his hands for silence, continued.

"No flavor may be refused. The 26 flavors may be eaten in any order, but all bits and pieces, including nuts and dough balls, must be eaten. In the event of Meltdown, all liquid must be consumed. Regulation time will be thirty minutes. In the event of a tie there will be one overtime period of 10 minutes and 10 scoops. If still tied each duelist will challenge the other to a Sudden Death Sundae of his choice."

With great pomp and circumstance the Manager of the Emporium and his assistant brought forth two large glass boats filled with 26 scoops. The duelists lifted their large spoons, poised for action.

"On your mark," shouted The Snort. "Get Ready! EAT!"

A cheer reverberated throughout the Mall as GG and Freckles quickly dipped into the mountain of ice cream before them. GG began with vanilla then proceeded to chocolate and strawberry, never hesitating between flavors. Freckles began with flavors he didn't like, saving his favorites for last.

Rocky Road, Marshmallow Yellow, Raspberry Sherbet, Peanut Butter Surprise. Scoop after scoop disappeared. Seconds wiped sweat from brows. It was fast. It was furious. The crowd watched first GG then Freckles. They cheered each scoop completed, and marveled at the speed with which each duelist ate. At the fifteen-minute mark the Challenger was even with the Champ.

On and on they ate. Cookies 'n Cream, Strawberry Sherbet, Lemon Meringue Pie, Peppermint Crunch, Pralines 'n Cream, Butter Nut, Tangerine Ice, Chocolate Crunch, Cinnamon 'n Raisin, Coconut Swirl, Jamoca Almond Fudge, Vanilla Malt, Vanilla Bean, French Vanilla Supreme.

A hush fell over the spectators as the duelists began to slow down. Amazingly, it was GG who first showed signs of slipping. Twice he lost the grip on his spoon.

Suddenly Freckles stopped mid-slurp, looked up, swallowed hard, then belched rather inelegantly. So startled was GG that he lost a bite as his spoon tipped. GG had been slightly ahead, but now did the unthinkable. He glanced at the Challenger, hesitating just enough to allow Freckles to catch up. They were scoop for scoop and spoon for spoon. Just as they both swallowed that last spoonful of Peach Melba, The Snort called time.

"Dead even," he proclaimed. "The Overtime period will begin after a short break."

The Emporium's manager and his assistant built two more mounds of ice cream, 10 scoops each. The Champ and the Challenger stood to stretch their muscles. The Champ quietly loosened his belt. The Challenger sloshed water around in his mouth and expectorated into the bucket.

The crowd murmured and shifted for better positions. No one could believe it. The Champ had never needed overtime to beat an opponent.

Ten scoops each and 10 minutes later The Snort called time again.

"Dead even," he shouted. The crowd went crazy.

Good old Freckles was even with the Champ! Amazing. Exciting. Too good to be true.

"Attention," The Snort yelled over the din. "The challengers have authorized the following for the Sudden Death Sundae finale." A hush fell over the crowd. "The Champ challenges the Challenger to eat the Double-double Delight, with pineapple sauce, whipped cream, nuts and a cherry."

"OO-OO-OO!" Brigitte cringed. But Freckles just nodded.

The Snort continued. "The Challenger challenges the Champ to eat a Double-double Toil and Trouble with Chocolate Chocolate-chip Cookie Dough ice cream, hot fudge, whipped cream and a cherry."

"Oh, wow!" The crowd murmurs echoed the thoughts of the Champ's Seconds. "Gordon hates that ice cream," Gwynn muttered.

At the signal the duelists dug in. Slowly they ate, each watching the other, daring him to quit. GG seemed to slump lower and lower over the table. Freckles groaned twice as he chewed the nuts. Slower and slower. Their arms grew weary, their jaws slackened, their teeth ached from the cold. Finally, neither could go on. The duel . . . was over.

The Emporium's Manager and his assistant took the sundae glasses to the counter, poured the remaining contents into separate containers and weighed each one. The crowd, the duelists, the Referee and the Seconds waited breathlessly for the verdict. The Manager handed the results to The Snort.

"Ladies and Gentlemen," the Referee began, "The Champion Ice Cream Eater of Haddleyville High is . . . Freckles Fremont!"

The crowd cheered wildly as Freckles stood in the midst of his admirers and beamed. Twice he belched, but was immediately forgiven. He was the Champ after all.

Gracious in defeat, Gorgeous Gordon accepted his loss, giving praise to a worthy successor. And in their Senior year GG again won the State Heavy – weight Wrestling Championship, then cheered Freckles to victory in the State Fair Ice Cream Challenge.

The repercussions were awesome and are still felt today. Jocks root for the Debate Team. The Chess Club sponsors Football Pep Rallies. Golf Teams request statistical data from the Math Club. The students of Haddleyville High cheer all accomplishments, still give each other weird nicknames and remember fondly those heroes of yesteryear.

Biography of
Michael Murphy

Michael J. Murphy, a graduate of North Eastern University in Boston, was an editorial assistant at the Boston Globe Newspaper, a television producer for many years at WBZ-TV, also in Boston, the NBC affiliate.

Later he owned and operated an advertising agency and film production company. A former Army officer, he served as an intelligence staff officer in the Washington D. C. area and later as a NATO international staff officer working outside Paris.

Michael was born and raised in Gardiner, Maine.

CAFÉ' JACQUES

Fiction

by Michael Murphy

Professor Harry Sinclair is on loan to Harvard University for a period of two years. To him, the relocation represents a sabbatical of sorts, interrupting fourteen consecutive years of teaching, lecturing and writing at his native Oxford University.

What prompted the move was a book entitled Italian Renaissance Art, a volume authored by Sinclair and widely distributed in academic circles. Plaudits for the work were universal, the most important critiques appearing in the Sunday book review sections of both the London Times and the New York Times newspapers.

Favorable reviews translated into brisk sales, well beyond the publisher's expectations. Within three months, it had become abundantly clear that the book would be going into a second printing. As a consequence, the professor was vaulted from relative obscurity to the front ranks of international fame.

For one to appreciate the success of Italian Renaissance Art, one must first observe the physical volume as it appeared in bookstores to the purchasing public. Fourteen inches tall and eleven and a half inches wide, its dust cover featuring a fountain with water gushing at full bloom, the photograph shot slightly out of focus in order to blend with the white lettering in the title as well as the author's name. The fountain itself dominated an ancient Italian Town Square, suggesting the outpouring of creative effort realized by artists, sculptors and architects during the celebrated era.

Praise for what the London Times called his 'illuminating profile technique', Sinclair's work was complemented by more than one hundred-fifty beautifully rendered color photographs. The blend of visual mastery combined with the professor's lean, hard narrative, gave the public assurance that the expensive volume was worth the money paid for it.

The early success of Italian Renaissance Art got an additional boost from an unexpected quarter. Producers at BBC decided to chronicle the book's success, including an interview with Sinclair and his wife Lydia. The end result of the hour-long television documentary after two showings, sales of the book quadrupled. First edition copies became collector's treasures. Harry and Lydia Sinclair became instant celebrities.

The handsome intellectual Sinclair gained favor through his understated speaking style. Lydia Sinclair's performance was equally compelling, revealing, among other things, that all photographs had been done by her, with the original pictures used in slide presentations by her husband throughout the British Isles and the European Continent.

The Sinclairs became the darlings of the print media and they walked in the fierce light of public exposure. Yet all was not sweetness and light in their lives. Behind the trappings of fame and fortune, there were philosophical and dangerous psychological differences that threatened their relationship. Divorce had become a distinct possibility.

Having discussed their dilemma, the Sinclairs opted to accept the trip to America. On one hand, the move would help them escape the public limelight. Secondly, the two year visit would afford them ample time to rehabilitate their marriage.

Preparations for the move were set in motion. They would leave on a BOAC flight from Heathrow Airport on a Sunday evening in mid-August. When all the arrangements were in place, a bedroom incident involving Lydia and a young man threw a giant wrench into the departure plan. The trouble had occurred two days before their scheduled take-off and it happened while the Sinclairs were hosting a farewell party.

Two months later, Harry Sinclair hurriedly walking a macadam path through the high walled sanctum that is Harvard Yard, was deep in thought. "Curious", he said to himself, "that the anti-Viet Nam war protesters had not yet invaded this magical place." Dressed in the bright colored leaves of autumn, the 'yard' remained remarkably undisturbed, unlike Harvard Square itself which the night before had been the scene of rioting. In spite of his disgust for the destruction around him, Sinclair, nodded and smiled as people passed, relishing the fact that he was among elite company, a working professor at what was possibly the finest educational institution in the entire Western World.

He ducked through an open gate and struggled forward amidst foot and motor traffic toward the famous kiosk. In the process, his thoughts turned to Lydia and the fact that he was still not sleeping in the marital bed. During their farewell party a few weeks ago, she had dropped out of sight and he had gone looking for her. Opening an upstairs bedroom door where coats and guest paraphernalia were stored, there Lydia stood in a passionate embrace with an Oxford soccer player, the man's hand inside her dress massaging her buttocks.

Stunned, but fighting to contain his dignity, he said. "Lydia, there are guests downstairs who require your attention." Turning to the man, he added, "As for you, gather up your things and get out of my house!"

At the kiosk, he bought a copy of the London Times. While scanning the headlines, he overheard a middle age patron speaking to the kiosk owner. "So my barber, he gets his kid back from Viet Nam in a body bag. And guess what? He don't know whether the body in that bag is his kid, or not. How'd you like to plan for that funeral?"

Sinclair absorbed the information with sadness for the grieving father, yet appalled at the man's ignorance of the English language.

Finally entering the Café Jacques, a loud emotional exchange aroused his curiosity. They sat on the short end of the bar facing one another. The man, younger than the woman.

Sinclair paused, arranging his Rex Harrison hat on a wooden peg near the door.

"What gets me is the damned duplicity of this thing! I mean, if it was just my wife, I could handle it. But my son, he's nine years old. When I look him in the eye, I think of you and me and I feel like a hypocrite." His voice grew louder. "I can't stand it! That's why this thing between us has got to end!"

The woman who had been sobbing, brought a cocktail napkin to her eyes. Struggling for composure, she replied. "Oh, for God's sake, Tim! What we have is something special and it does not, I repeat not, intrude upon your home life!"

By this time, Sinclair had moved half way up the long side of the bar and sat down.

Winking at the bar tender, Emile, neither spoke as they listened to the quarreling couple.

The woman's voice had turned shrill. "Jesus Christ, your conscience attack is pure bull. The truth of your situation is this: You're away from home. You're on the road and we are consenting adults!" She paused, "And, thanks to you, my makeup is a mess. You'll have to excuse me." She slid off the bar stool and headed around the bar in the direction of the ladies room.

Sinclair smiled as the bartender spoke. "Bon jour, mon professeur. Comment ce va?"

"C'est va bien, Emile. Today I would like to order your wonderful spinach quiche and with it, a pot of Earl Grey tea."

"Immediately." Emile hit a small bell, signaling a waitress from the kitchen. A minute later, he placed a pot of steaming tea with a cup and saucer in front of Sinclair.

"This tea, as you may know," Emile said, "we keep here for one of our most special customers. It is you!"

Sinclair, unfolding the London Times, welcomed the tea. "I am most appreciative, mon ami."

"Bar keep!" The words sounded like a shot from the young man at the end of the bar. "Another round here. Strawberry daiquiri for the lady and for me, I'll switch to a bottle of Heiniken Beer."

"Right away, sir." Emile replied, swinging into action.

"Bloody noisy in the 'square' last night." Sinclair offered. "Protesters left a most untidy mess. Broken plate glass. Blood spattered about. Such destruction."

"Ah, yes." Emile countered. "it is a very big circus, protests all over the country. And the chief clown, Mr. Johnson. He sits in Washington and pretends not to hear."

"Your humor hits the mark", the professor replied. "Should President Johnson not heed their message, he may soon be packing his bags."

The blond woman returning from the ladies room, her makeup intact, passed Sinclair. He studied what he saw: Peroxide blond. Mini skirt cut to the crotch. White blouse unbuttoned at the top, featuring a see-through embroidery exposing her ample breasts.

Pretending to be absorbed in his newspaper, Sinclair and Emile leaned closer, making an attentive audience of two.

Returning to her seat, the blond woman spoke in an innocent conciliatory voice. "Is this my goodbye drink?" She exhibited renewed charm and poise.

Her companion responded in kind. "I prefer to think of it as a toast" He raised his bottle, saluting her. "To days of Victorian splendor," he declared.

"Oh sir, your words," she replied with wide-eyed innocence. "They are enough to make a young girl blush." She crossed her legs, bringing her cocktail glass to her mouth, closing her lips around the straw, drawing the bright liquid through a bank of crushed ice.

"Madam may recall our most recent rendezvous." At this point, he lowered his voice.

Halfway up the bar, the fascinate audience of two strained to hear better.

"That thin piece of rope with knots in it," the young man's voice had turned confidential. "I mean, Holy Christ, I've never experienced anything like that!"

She smiled at him, now exuding charm and confidence. "The toy, sir, to which you refer is, I do believe of Japanese manufacture. Not, if you please, to be confused with things Victorian."

"Whatever its origin," he sighed. "I shall never forget the effect it produced!" He picked up his beer bottle and raised it to his lips, then chug-a-lug style he drank it empty and smacked the bottle down on the bar with a resounding thug.

"Oh sir," she spoke in a coquettish sigh. "Your manner of speaking confuses a young girl. I wonder what it is that you are trying to say?"

He leaned closer to her face, resting an elbow on the bar. "What I'm saying," he declared, "is all that stuff I complained about earlier, all of a sudden it seems trivial.

"What I say now, is it's about time that you and I get the hell out of this place."

Immediately, she was on her feet fetching a mirror to again shore up her makeup. She slipped on an expensive trench coat that had been draped on her stool. Her companion stood beside her putting on his suit jacket and straightening his tie.

"The Roosevelt, is that okay?"

'The Roosevelt is fine. Try for the Victorian Suite."

"Consider it done", he answered emphatically. Then fetching two crumpled twenty dollar bills from his pocket, he waved at Emile. "Food. Drinks. Tip!" he turned to the blond and said with a smile, "We're out of here!"

Within seconds, they were out the door

Professor Sinclair looked across the bar at Emile. "That couple – they do not appear to be overly concerned about the war protestors."

Laughing, Emile said. "Pas de toute!, Monsieur professeur The man, I would say, is about one discreet tip away from getting what he desires."

Laughing also, Sinclair nodded his agreement. Pouring more tea into his cup, he added a splash of cream. Looking toward the door where the couple had exited, his thoughts turned to Lydia. That morning at breakfast she had announced that she had an appointment for a massage. Sinclair had not inquired whether the masseur was a male, or. female. The image of his wife's oiled and naked body being rubbed and massaged by male hands, made him ill. Sinclair felt a hotness at the back of his neck that spread up to his ears.

A massage, he grumbled to himself. That will be an issue at our next therapy session. Sinclair and Lydia were seeing a psychiatrist, a balding, effeminate man whom the professor despised.

Biography of
Kenneth J. Bradeen

Ken Bradeen served as Chief of Police of Norwell, Massachusetts for twenty-five years. He later served another five years as Deputy Collector of Taxes. He was an advisor to Massasoit College for its Law Enforcement program. Ken also taught Seamanship and Navigation, he spent vacations sailing the New England coast with his wife in his 28' sailboat, and after retirement sailed in the Bahamas.

He retired in 1978 and has lived in Florida since 1980.

Ken and his wife, Beulah have three children, six grand children and nine great-grand children.

Other than personal letters and police reports, Ken says he never wrote before becoming involved with The Villages Writers Group.

EUREKA!

Fiction

by Ken Bradeen

In the small fishing village where he lived, he was known as a nice fellow. His name was Tom Nelson, age twenty-five and a graduate of Boston University with a bachelors in political science. A nagging regret at this point in his life was uncertainty over his career choice. Was it possible he was wasting his time and life working as a lobsterman? Would his parents be devastated if he went elsewhere? Shouldn't he go, anyway.

As usual, the alarm clock went off at four-thirty. It was still dark on this mid-coast Maine morning in June. Reluctantly he got out of bed and put on his working clothes, clean ones today. Usually he got two day's wear out of a set of dungarees and a wool flannel shirt, but fish crud as he baited lobster traps often found the front of his clothing and had to be washed as soon as he left his boat.

After completing his toilet and filling a thermos, he checked the refrigerator to search for something edible. Oh yes, the beef stew his mother had delivered yesterday and the homemade bread from Jean would do nicely.

Jean Kingsley was John's latest heartthrob. They had met a few weeks back when he had driven to Camden to seek a better market for his lobsters as his local co-op had stopped paying the market price. Jean had been on his mind all week. Tom was beginning to realize that he'd been playing the field long enough. No way had he considered settling down with any of the flighty young women that had sexually excited him. Jean was different. She was a graduate of the University of Maine and a teacher at the Baxter Elementary School. A year older than John, they had enjoyed each other's company, but there was a bit of a problem in their religious affiliations – one that would be difficult to present to both sets of parents. Yet, he was crazy about his new love and thought about her most hours of the day.

With continuing pleasant thoughts of Jean, John left his house and drove his pickup the short distance to the dock where a skiff waited to be rowed out to his mooring. Before leaving the cove, John loaded a barrel of bait onto his workboat Betsey. The old Ford diesel started on command and all was well with his world as he cast off, setting the tach at 1500 rpm. As usual his old friend, a gull with a crooked leg sat perched on his radar mast. John smiled and threw the bird a fish, wondering if the crooked leg had been caught in ice during one hard winter years ago. Now he cleared the harbor and rounded the point, observing two other boats just ahead in the semi-dark of a new breaking dawn. He urged the throttle up to 1800. That would get him soon to his first string of pots. With his new GPS, finding his traps was no longer a hit or miss operation. He had pre-programmed the unit to go directly to each string, saving time and annoyance, especially in poor visibility.

Although the locals were in competition for lobsters, in reality they were like a big family, always ready and willing to help one another. John picked up his phone and said, "Good Morning, Dave." to the owner of the boat a half mile ahead. His friend's answer, a raspy grunt, suggested that Dave was a bit hung over. John chuckled. He'd been in the same fix a couple times.

The morning continued as usual without any serious problems. He decided to leave his pots on the far side of the island and maybe they would produce better the next day. His catch today had been so-so, not good, but enough to make expenses. That was important. His semi-annual insurance was due in a week and a gas bill from May. He usually settled up with the cooperative every two weeks. They paid his running expenses and deducted the funds from the amount they owed him.

As Tom came upon the last string of pots, he noticed a floating box, or something unusual, almost dead ahead. Turning into the wind, he decided to have a look. The object appeared to be a small suitcase, or brief case that was just barely floating. He grabbed a boat hook and tried to snag the handle. It took several tries, but finally he hauled the heavy, water laden, leather case into his boat. Almost on top of his floats, he hauled in all ten strings before coming about and heading for home.

On the route back to the dock, he took a closer look at the mysterious object that had obviously been in the water for some time. Unable to open the locked clasp, he cut the leather with his 'pig sticker,' then pulled the top back. Tom let out a yell, "Oh, my God."

What he saw was neatly packaged layers of plastic-covered money. Although nearly opaque, he could make out a stack of $100 dollar bills and another of $50's. They had been tightly wrapped and appeared to be dry inside. When his heart rate subsided, he quickly scanned the horizon to see if he'd been observed by any nearby boats. None were close, so he assumed that he'd not been seen.

What should I do now, he thought. If he carried the heavy case from his boat up to the dock, everyone on the dock would want to know what he had found. Yet, he hated to leave all that money on his boat. His mind was a flurry of anxiety. He needed a plan and some time to think. He was eight miles from the harbor. That meant he had little over a half hour to figure out what to do next.

Just after noon, the wind came and the water began to get choppy. Not worried about a little spray and some pounding, he decided to leave the suitcase on board until dark and slip back later on some pretext and retrieve it. He placed the wet bag in the fo'c's'le and piled some oilskins on top, plus a folder of old charts he intended to take home to scotch tape the rips.

Tom picked up his mooring and made everything fast. His emotions would not allow him to act normal, but he had to try. His mind wandered back to the day a couple years back when he was stern man on Bill Shaw's boat. They had come upon a floating body and had radioed the Coast Guard in somewhat of a panic. They were ordered to stand by until a cutter came out from Boothbay. A traumatic moment, but so different from his present panic.

Back then, Tom had looked forward to walking up the ramp to greet the assembling crowd and tell them what had happened. By the time they got ashore, radio and TV reporters from as far away as Portland were waiting to talk with them. Tom remembered that it was fun being a celebrity, even for a moment.

Today was dramatically different. He must be as inconspicuous as possible. Avoid attention, or questions. It would be stressful returning to his house and waiting until dark before he could retrieve the suitcase and count his newly – found treasure, but that appeared to be the safest plan. He agonized. *How much money could be enclosed in that sized container? Where did it come from? Was it drug money some criminal under chase by law enforcement boats had tossed overboard?* All sorts of fantasies crowded his over wrought mind. Perhaps the money was ransom for a fairy princess. The next few hours of waiting and delay would be pure misery.

Should he phone Jean? Should he notify his parents? What to do! It was mid afternoon. The dock looked clear. So far, so good. Tom tied up the boat, checked the shutoff, no longer trusting the automatic bilge pump To protect his boat from a dead battery. He couldn't resist taking one more look at his hidden fortune, then lowered his catch into the skiff and headed for the lobster-receiving vehicle at the south end of the dock.

It was the warmest time of the day, yet he was covered with goose bumps and he found it difficult to hide his shaking hands as he dumped his catch and replaced the hatch cover of the co-op's hatch cover. It was just sixty feet to the dock, but during this short row, he literally kicked himself for not hiding at least one package of the money inside his lunch box. It would have been exciting to count it at home. Too late now. He strained to go about his usual business, but his mind continued to reel. *Should he call his dad, or Jean, or both?* The thought did not lend itself to an instant decision. When he pulled into his yard, Tom noticed his neighbor Charlie, a fellow fisherman, already home and working in his garden.

"Hi, Charlie. How'd it go today?" Tom smiled, pleased that he could sound normal.

"Not too good," his neighbor grumbled. "Had a skip in my motor.

Thought I might have to call you for a tow, but I nursed the old tug home. I'll have to take off tomorrow and pull the plugs – run some carburetor cleaner through her. Maybe I'll get lucky and avoid having to call Mac. His rates have gone through the ceiling."

"Yeah, I heard that he wants to retire at fifty with a million bucks," Tom added, trying to appear interested in the defective carburetor.

"Better luck tomorrow. See ya."

Bouncing up the stairs to his house, he unlocked his front door, then locked it again. Usually this was a time for a cold beer, but today he needed something stronger. Out came a bottle of Scotch. He knew his dad would be home, but Jean had to work until four-fifteen. Not wishing to cloud his thinking, he poured a modest drink and sat down for some serious thought. *What were his options? Marriage? Travel? Back to school for a Master's Degree? Decisions, decisions.*

His life was before him and it was fun to fantasize about all the exotic places that had been only dreams. With lots of money, the possibilities were endless. Feeling a bit mellow from the drink, he began to accept his new found wealth as his due.

He and Jean had an understanding that week nights were not date nights. She worked long hours and needed time to prepare for her next day's work as a teacher. Normally, Tom accepted the common sense of her schedule, but to phone his dad tonight and not Jean, would exclude her from the excitement of his news. This would hurt her, perhaps even impair their relationship. Of course, he was an independent adult and close to his parents, but no way did he want to hurt her feelings.

By now, it was five-thirty. If he phoned his parent's house, his mother would insist that he come for dinner. He couldn't ask his dad to go down to the boat with him without also inviting his mother. Finally, it came to him. He'd tell his father that he needed a new hauler and wanted some advice on how to hook it up. Tom would pick up his dad at six-thirty when it would be near dark. They could row out to the boat and retrieve the loot. On the way out, Tom would have time to tell his dad the entire story. *Yes, this was a good plan.*

Now for Jean. If she was to be included in his future, she had to be informed immediately. Forget busy schedules.

"Hello Jean, guess who?"

"Hi yourself. Anything wrong? I didn't expect a call from you tonight."

"I know. Nothing drastic, but something came up today and I need to ask your opinion. I don't mean to sound mysterious, but I don't wish to discuss the matter on the phone, or on the internet. Can you drop by my house about seven?"

"Gee Hon, you know how busy I am and what little free time I have during the week. I still have two hours of exams to correct before tomorrow's class. Is it really important?"

"I respect that, but this time I really need you for just a little while." *I need you,* worked every time.

"Okay, if it's that important – but I can't stay very long," she said.

"Thanks Jean, you won't regret it."

Mother didn't quite know what to make of his call, but good old Dad was always ready for anything. Tom was not hungry, but had some time to kill and he did have one more "You Heat" dinner in the freezer.

At six-thirty he picked up his dad and in a few minutes they were at the skiff. He had wanted his father to stay in the pickup, but that would destroyed his excuse for getting him out. They both slid into the damp seats of the skiff.

"What's the matter with your hauler? I thought it was new last year when you bought this piece of junk." Tom's father always belittled the boat as not worth the price.

"Come down into the cabin and I will show you the plans," Tom said, turning on the single cabin light He pulled back the covering exposing the old leather case with the hole he had cut in the top.

At this moment Tom was not the only one to show excitement. "What in the Hell have you come up with now?" his father muttered.

"I found this floating today – just look!" Tom removed the covering.

"Holy Mackerel!" Tom Sr. exclaimed. "Where did you find this?"

"It was floating off Spruce Point, just out of the channel and . . ."

His father didn't wait for further explanations, "God Almighty, there must be a million dollars there," he said, lifting one of the packages.

Tom put back the package his father had picked up. "I can't even guess how much is in there, we'll have to take it back to the house to count it."

Tom had never seen his father in such a lather. He was so excited he talked constantly asking over and over just how he had found such a treasure.

"Please Dad, you know how voices carry over the water. Hold it down until we get back to the house." His father's excitement had rekindled his own, and they both had difficulty getting into the skiff and rowing back to the dock The warning didn't dampen the older man's excitement and he continued to chatter.

"Dad, I know you and Mother are not happy with the girl I've been seeing the past few months." said Tom on the way back to the house in the pickup. "But she's special to me. I love her and we don't dwell on our religious differences. We both worship God, so when there are children, I'm sure we're going to be mature enough to work it all out. I have confidence that when mother spends some time with Jean, she will love her, too. So, before you say anything, I want you to know that I've asked Jean to come over to the house tonight to be part of the excitement."

For once Tom Sr. had nothing to say!

Jeans car was in the yard when Tom pulled into the drive. He had given her a house key on the second date, so she was already inside. Tom took the case wrapped in oilskins into the house. Jean seemed uneasy when she saw Tom Sr. follow his son through the front door.

"Hi Jean, you've met my dad. Let's sit down and I'll tell you everything that's happened. First, I am going to put this package into the bedroom just in case we have unexpected company." Jean remained calm until she had heard of Tom's discovery, and soon she became as excited as Tom Sr. when they went into the bedroom and opened the soaking wet leather case. Fortunately the packs of currency were so well wrapped that the water had not yet seeped in. The money was dry. The count showed eight packets across, and three deep. Twenty-four packets of bills in all. The next important count was the number and denomination of the bills contained in each package.

They each took a package and started to count. It was easy to lose count with so many crisp bills at hand. The bills were in denominations of hundreds, fifties and twenties. They determined that each package contained bills totaling ten thousand dollars.

"God, that's a total of two hundred and forty thousand!" said Tom.
It was now nine-fifteen. Tom knew his mother would be frantic, so he wasn't surprised when the phone rang.

"Yes, Mother, I'll bring Dad home shortly. No, we're not drunk. Yes, I know I sound excited, Dad will tell you all about it when he gets home. No, I can't tell you over the phone. Be patient a little while longer. Good night, Mother."

"Look everyone," he said to Jean and his father, "no matter how pent up inside you are, please don't tell anyone about the money. We have some serious thinking to do before we say anything. You know the newspapers and TV will have a field-day over this. First we have to check the law. I think there's a federal statute that requires a person to turn in 'found money' over a certain amount. So, let's keep this to ourselves as long as possible."

Jean rode along with Tom when he drove his father back to his house. "I don't think it'll be possible to get any sleep tonight." she said.

Tom's dad invited them in while he told his wife the news. "Otherwise she'll keep you on the phone the rest of the night".

It was over an hour and two cups of coffee later before they were able to leave. Now four people knew the secret. *How long would it take before someone spilled the beans?* Tom wondered.

"Forget the exams I was going to correct, I'm too excited to go home tonight."

"Sure, stay overnight." Tom was delighted.

Jean had always been careful not to leave her car in the yard overnight. "You know how people gossip." But tonight she ignored all precautions. There were serious questions requiring answers. And, it didn't take much persuading to have Jean call in sick when morning arrived.

There had been little sleep that night. Tired as he was he decided that he'd better continue his regular routine to avoid having to answer questions such as, "What's going on, Tom?" Jean agreed. In the back of both of their minds was the thought that they needed time to search their innermost concerns and their future relationship.

Jean made a special breakfast for Tom, then he was off to work. After cleaning up the kitchen, she sat down. Tears came easily as she asked for divine guidance. In retrospect she thought her life was satisfying Tom, being the more impetuous type would surely want to chase a few rainbows before settling down. *Maybe that's what she needed to fill in the emptiness of her teaching life.* She would be twenty-seven in two months with no prospects of the American dream – a handsome husband in a profession, a three bedroom house overlooking the ocean, a fancy car in the garage, two children and a dog. Other than when some of the summer vacationers appeared, there were few local prospects with anything close to those credentials. She knew that Tom could be somewhat irresponsible, bordering on immaturity at times, but he had a good work ethic, was not a heavy drinker, never smoked and could be trusted.

Getting back to reality, she no longer could refrain from just another peek at all that money, Tom had put in the closet. She opened a package once again as a thought occurred; it would be a good idea if she researched the law to find out the ramifications of 'found money'. She was sure that he I.R.S. would frown on such activity.

Tom had gone through the motions of rowing out to the boat, firing up old Betsey and heading out to the fishing grounds. All this was done without giving too much thought to details. A light breeze from the nor'east brought on the usual change to sou'west just after noon. Sometimes it brought strong winds with a heavy chop. He called a couple of his fishing buddies, more to establish an alibi than show any interest in conversation.

His mind was exhausted, and now the adventurous quirks of his nature began to take over. What if he confessed to Jean that he wasn't ready to settle down? The possibilities had him dreaming things that would have embarrassed his parents. Imagine flying to Miami or Key West, buying a houseboat and living the life of a Bon Vivant! If he got bored he could always sign on as crew on a dragger or shrimper. Other possibilities were worth considering, such as going abroad or doing the South Seas. He thought of sailing the Pacific Islands with stops at Tahiti, Fiji or Bora Bora – he could easily get a passport and travel documents.

After heading to the far side of the island that he had missed hauling yesterday, he headed back to the harbor. It was starting to cloud over and rain was imminent. While not giving up the dreams of earlier in the day entirely, he realized that he could not alienate himself from his parents and friends, especially Jean.

When he returned to his cottage there was no car, Jean was out doing errands, he assumed. After a shower, he dressed in his best suit and shined his LL Bean's specials. He debated whether to have a quick libation or not. He decided against it. He had invited Jean to join him for dinner at a fine restaurant on the dock at East Boothbay

A little after five, Jean arrived at his cottage. Immediately he knew something was wrong. She was flushed and by her walk it was obvious that she had something to say. And it wasn't good. "Sweetheart," she began, "I have a confession to make and I have to apologize. I did some thinking this morning and called the police without identifying myself and asked what the laws are regarding finding cash. They informed me that it was against the law not to declare it and turn it over. If, however, it was found to be legitimate and not derived from drug money or stolen, it would be returned to te finder after one year."

"Okay," said Tom,"that's no big deal to get flustered over."

"But that's not all," she stammered. "Maybe you'd better sit down when I tell you the worse part."

Now Tom became apprehensive. "There's more?"

"I'm afraid so. I also went to the bank to see Mary, my old roommate. She works there."

"Oh, God, why would you do that?" he demanded.

"Here's what happened. After you left this morning, I got to thinking and asked myself, what if this all fell apart at the seams?"

"So, why was Mary brought into this and what did you tell her?" Tom's anger was beginning to show.

"Trust me Tom. I just told her that I was given the bills in change for some furniture I bought at an auction and that they just didn't feel right, I swore her to secrecy. Well, Mary took the bills into a back room and put them under some kind of black light. They are counterfeit!"

There was an ominous silence before he spoke. "Jean," he said, "dreams come and go, some dreams materialize, but most don't. This has left me with no doubt that I love you and I have two questions. The first is, will you marry me and the second, where did I put that damned alarm clock?"

Biography of
Omah MacDonald Kiser

Omah Kiser was born in West Palm Beach, Florida. Majoring in psychology at the University of Florida for three years. She left college in Gainesville to marry a *country Boy*. She spent the next thirty-five years living on the edge of the Florida Everglades. She is the mother of two children, a boy and a girl.

While near the Everglades she managed a walk-in/hot-line for those with mental problems. When her husband died she moved from the Everglades and as she says, *rejoined civilization.*

Because of her years of isolated living, she felt herself an *odd man out*, but found the easiest way to explain her attitudes was to write little stories about things that happened in her life. Omah writes under the name McDonald. The following memoirs present a few hilarious events of her life and those around her.

MOTHER AND THE TOMATO JUICE

Memoir

by Omah Katherine MacDonald

We moved to Singer Island, Florida, toward the end of my junior year in high-school. The word that can best describe our whole family situation is, "Chaotic!" By the time I went off to college, things had settled into a sort of routine, and my mother had decided to take a little time for her own enjoyment. She scheduled a once a-week appointment at a local weight reduction center and also helped organize a weekly afternoon bridge club. Although she was very warm and out-going, mother was a lady down to the tips of her toes. When she went out in the afternoon, she always wore a hat, stockings, high heals, and short, white gloves. She was slightly overweight, but impeccably groomed, with nothing wrinkled, disheveled or messy about her. This is the way she was dressed to go to her bridge club one Thursday afternoon.

Singer Island was mostly undeveloped land with one long, narrow, winding road that traversed its full length. Driving around a bend in this road, mother had the misfortune to surprise a skunk. It ran off the road, but sprayed her right front tire in retaliation for its fright. The smell was overpowering.

A few yards further down the road stood the island's first, and only, grocery store. Turning off the main, winding road, mother pulled up to the curb, cut off the motor, and went inside. As most of the customers wore casual clothing, she was greeted by the owner who, with a smile, asked if he could be of any assistance.

"Yes," replied mother, "I really need a large can of tomato juice."

"Oh! We have that," he said, "Let me show you where it is."

After she had chosen the largest can she could find, he escorted her to the check-out counter, where she bought the juice. Then she asked if they could open it for her.

"Of course," said the clerk, "But wouldn't you rather have a cold can? We have some in the refrigerated section."

"No, thank you," mother said, "this is exactly what I need."

The grocer, having waited through this exchange, escorted mother out the door, asked her to come again, and stood there to see her off.

Mother walked up to her tire and proceeded to completely cover it with the tomato juice. When she had finished, she bent down and smelled the tire. Straightening up, she shook her head in the universal "No" signal and returned to the store.

The grocer, who was still standing by his entrance, opened the door for her and escorted her back into the store. "Is there anything else?" he asked.

"Yes," said mother, "I'm going to need another can of tomato juice."

"Why don't I go get it for you?" he suggested.

"That would be very nice," mother replied.

When he returned with the juice, the clerk rang up the sale, and then asked her if she wanted to have this can of warm juice also opened.

"Thank you," mother said, "I would appreciate it."

The grocer again escorted mother out of the store. This time, the clerk followed along. As they both stood outside the store, mother approached her car, but then she noticed a small pothole in the street just in front of her parked car. She filled this pothole with her tomato juice, and then got back into her car and proceeded to drive back and forth through the pothole several times. Finally she got out of her car, came around the car to her tire, bent over and smelled it again. With another shake of her head, she headed back into the store.

This time, the proprietor held the door open for her, and the clerk volunteered to fetch the tomato juice.

"No, Mary," said the owner, "go back to your station. Freddy," he called to the back for the stock boy, "Why don't you bring us a large can of tomato juice from aisle three?" Freddy brought the juice, watched as the clerk rang up the sale and opened the can. Then he walked out the door with mother, the clerk and the owner to see her off.

Another customer had arrived, parked in front of mother, and was in the process of getting out of his car. Mother approached his side of his car and knocked on his window.

"Mister," she said, "You have parked right over a nice little pothole. I have been filling it with tomato juice, and I have just gotten some more. I wonder if you would be kind enough to pull ahead a little bit so that I can fill it again?"

"Sure," he said, "I'll be glad to, Lady, anything you want." He moved his car quite a distance ahead giving mother all the space she could possibly use, then he joined the small group in front of the store.

Mother filled her pothole and drove back and forth through it several times. After a few minutes, she got out of her car and again smelled her tire. As she was turning to go back into the store, another car parked behind her. She approached this car and asked this driver to back up a little, telling him how considerate the other customer had been. This driver glanced at the people gathered in front of the store, and backed way, way back. After locking his car securely, he also joined the group at the curb.

Mother, the owner, the clerk and the stock boy re-entered the store. The boy again fetched another can of warm juice. The clerk rang up the sale and opened the can. They all went outside where mother refilled the pothole and drove back and forth through it several times.

One more time, mother got out of her car, and bent down to smell her tire. This time, she nodded her head, "Yes." Re-entering her car, she acknowledged her audience with a graceful nod of her head; and then, with a regal flip of her gloved hand, drove away to her bridge game.

AUNT JEMIMAH STUBBS

When mother was five years old, her family lived next door to her father's furniture store. The front and side yards were enclosed with a fence, and the back yard also, but this was much larger, and included space for a barn and a storage shed. While the house wasn't elaborate or "showy" it was, "comfortable", with enough bedrooms for everyone, a nice, "parlor" in which my grandmother held, "Afternoon Teas," and had a wide porch running all the way around the house.

One afternoon, a stranger came in the gate while mother's father was home for lunch and asked if he could speak with him for a moment. Mother followed her father onto the porch, where the stranger remarked what a nice little girl she was. He then told mother's father that he would like to give this nice little girl his horse. He was sure that such a nice little girl would take very good care of his horse. My grandfather asked my mother if she thought she could take care of this man's horse.

"Oh! Yes," my mother replied. "Oh! I could take such good care of your horse."

And that is how my mother got Aunt Jemimah Stubbs.

My mother had a tapeworm when she was a young child and she was constantly eating. She and Aunt Jemimah Stubbs were a "Natural Pair." They were both constantly munching on carrots or apples or whatever else mother could find in the kitchen. Aunt Jemimah Stubbs followed her everywhere she went, and they both thoroughly enjoyed each other's company.

Mother was the only one that Aunt Jemimah Stubbs would allow on her back, and that would usually be for only a few minutes at a time. She would be walking forward and then take a quick side hop and mother would topple to the ground. Aunt Jemimah Stubbs would freeze in her tracks, and not take another step. She would reach her long neck around her foreleg and smell mother's face, and wait until mother got up on her feet, before moving away.

Mother always felt completely safe riding Aunt Jemimah Stubbs, and thought that smelling her face, was the horse's way of making sure that she was unhurt.

One day, grandmother was entertaining her friends at an afternoon tea. Mother's brother and sister were in school and mother was outside playing with Aunt Jemimah Stubbs. Mother got hungry. She decided to go into the kitchen to get a snack. Getting off of her horse at the front steps, she went inside and then into the kitchen. Aunt Jemimah also went up the steps, into the hallway, through the living room, into the dining room, completely around the dining room table, twice, then into the kitchen and out the back door. Mother claimed not to know that Aunt Jemimah was trailing behind her and never did understand why grandmother was upset.

About a year later, grandmother sent mother to the store with a message for grandfather. Mother forgot to close the front gate and Aunt Jemimah Stubbs followed her to the store. Mother entered the front door, wandered down the aisle of sofas and chairs, checked the office from there, and continued toward the back part of the store which is where the bedroom sets were kept. Here, the aisles were much more narrow, and certainly were never intended for a horse in the first place. She watched in horror as Aunt Jemimah Stubbs came to the end of the aisle and was confronted with a dressing table which was topped with a tall three-sectioned mirror.

Aunt Jemimah Stubbs did not have space to turn around. There was a dresser on her left side, a chest of drawers on her right, and this strange mirror directly in front of her. She reared up on her two hind legs, turned around in the opposite direction, keeping her forelegs above the encircling furniture, and landed back in the aisle without touching anything. My grandfather and his helper stood still, with their mouths hanging open. Aunt Jemimah Stubbs leisurely retraced her steps through the store, went out the front door and then home, my mother a few steps behind her. The message did not get delivered.

By now, Aunt Jemimah Stubbs was getting to be a very old horse, but she still had a surprise left in her. One day the circus came to town. This was a big event in my mother's small town. The train cars, that were owned by the circus, would be left on a siding at the train depot, and all of the tents and necessary paraphernalia would be marched through town in a parade. Not only did this fulfill the necessity of transporting everything to the fairground, but also served as advance publicity for the show.

Mother was riding Aunt Jemimah Stubbs in the back yard, when the circus came through town. I do not know whether she was being punished or whether there was simply no one to look after her; but she had been forbidden to go out on the street to watch the parade.

The music, of course, was the first thing you noticed as the parade approached. In the back yard, Aunt Jemimah started to prance. Down the street the Elephants led the parade. Then came some of the entertainers, with some of their crazy cars; then some of the caged animals; last, came the horses. Over the gate went Aunt Jemimah, mother on her back. Aunt Jemimah pranced, then when the music changed, Aunt Jemimah danced. She circled and she bowed. She followed the parade all the way to the fair grounds, dancing and prancing as well as any horse there. Mother, of course, was on her back all the way.

DRIVING WITH MOTHER

When we were married, Russ was managing a ranch in Boynton Beach. Named El Clair Ranch, it was situated on a shell road exactly one mile south of Boynton Road, and about 20 miles west of town. One of the ways you could get to Boynton Road was to go south from West Palm on an old highway called Military Trail.

Military Trail had a bad reputation when I was growing up in West Palm. There had been a lot of automobile accidents on that road; and two girls had been raped and murdered just off that road, and then dumped into a shell pit. This caused a great deal of uproar at that time. Eventually, the rapist – murderer was caught, tried and convicted.

When I got married, and moved to that area, my father asked me to avoid that road at all costs. Requests in my family were tantamount to orders and certainly to be obeyed. I tried to explain to my father that avoiding this road would be almost impossible, but this didn't cut any ice with him. He still insisted that if I cared about my safety, and about him I would not drive on that road. This was a Mexican standoff, and never was resolved.

We had been married about two years; when mother decided to drive down to see me one afternoon. Also, she decided to bring my niece, Jackie, with her. Jackie was then about three years old, and had a mind of her own. I really don't now why mother brought Jackie with her. They did not get along. Mother and Jackie's mother, Marion, did not get along, either. Mother always thought that Jackie was an "inconvenient" child, because she was born just after Don and Marion came to manage the Villas. It certainly was not the place for a baby. Of course, Jackie could not help when she was born.

Mother was not used to handling children. She had always had a maid or a nursemaid to look after us. Also, we were exceptionally obedient children. When we were told to do something – we did it.

Our luncheon went off very well. Jackie was on her best behavior and Omah Leah, who was only a couple of months' old, took her bottle, cooed and then fell asleep. We had had a nice visit, and I helped mother get Jackie back into the car. Mother then handed Jackie a cold can of Seven-up, which she had packed for the trip and they took off.

Now, mother had not promised daddy that she would not use the Trail, and this was the way she went home. They had only been on that road for a few miles when Jackie, who was standing in the front seat, rolled down her window, and threw her empty cola can out of it. Immediately, the policeman who was following them, hit his siren, and pulled mother over. She ended up parked right in front of the "Do not Litter, fine $500.00" sign.

Mother had never been stopped by a policeman before and was highly incensed that such a thing should happen to her. Most of the policemen in West Palm knew her, tipped their hat, and usually stopped traffic to allow her to drive wherever she wanted. She was a very much respected and appreciated member of our community.

This policeman didn't even tip his hat, nor did he say, "Good afternoon," to her, or address her as "Maam." "May I see your license?" he requested. Mother handed him her license. He read it and then asked her, "Did you throw that can out of your window?"

"No." said mother.

"Well," he said, "Someone did. I saw it come sailing out of your window."

"It was my granddaughter's drink. She must have thrown the can out of the window."

He looked at Jackie, then he walked back to the can, picked it up, and brought it back to the car. Jackie watched with interest. "Did you throw this out of the window?" he asked.

"Yes," said Jackie, very pleased with the attention she was getting.

Turning back to Mother, the policeman instructed her, "This is littering. Haven't you taught her not to do that?"

"She **is** my granddaughter." Said my mother, "But I leave her training to my son and my daughter-in-law."

"Nevertheless," replied the policeman, "she is a passenger in your car, and you should see to it that the laws are not broken."

Mother said nothing. She had never been reprimanded by a policeman before. Then he said, "I will not give you a ticket this time. You must be more careful in the future." He handed her the can, then returned to his patrol car.

Mother took a minute to gather her wits about her, handed the offending can to Jackie, and started her car.

Jackie, who was still standing in the front seat next to mother, grinned, and turning to the still open window, and again threw the can out again.

SHOULD I ADD?

Once more the policeman got out of his car, this time slamming his door, retrieved the can and silently gave it to mother. Mother didn't say anything either. Jackie never went anywhere with mother again.

Biography of
Marcia Reisman

Marcia Reisman and her husband came to the Villages from Port St. Lucie, Florida. She writes delightful memoirs of her family, in particular, her grandmother, Bubbe Dear, whose treasure of wisdom and life philosophy gave Marcia material for many stories and life's adventures.

BUBBE DEAR

Memoir

by Marcia Reisman

Bubbe Dear had been blessed with many talents. If anyone became ill she had the cure – usually hot chicken soup and a mustard plaster. She could also bake strudels and bread using her own method of measuring – a pinch of this, a palm full of that. But to me her best talent was story-telling. She was my mother's mother. I didn't learn her true name until I was too old to believe in fairy tales – Bubbe Dear's fairy tales. I was a true believer and her most attentive audience any time she said, "A long time ago in the old country . . . ."

Every Friday morning I would accompany Bubbe Dear to the butcher. In back of his shop he had a chicken coop. The chickens squawked and ran around the little fenced in area and Bubbe Dear would study them for a few minutes then point to a fat healthy hen and say, "That one!" Then we would go into the small stall at the back of the shop, the one with the chicken feathers all over the floor, and wait for the butcher to bring us the slain bird.

The little stall had a stool and a gas burner with a small flame. Bubbe Dear would sit and pluck the feathers from the bird, and I would gather the feathers together in a soft pile. I liked the feel of the soft white feathers. When she had finished plucking the hen Bubbe Dear would hold the chicken into the flame to burn off any tiny pinfeathers that were left. Then the butcher would wrap up the chicken and off we would go, home again, to cook the bird for our Sabbath dinner.

One Friday I asked, "Bubbe Dear, why does the butcher take the chicken out back where no one can see or hear him?"

"My precious," she explained, "if the butcher doesn't slay the chicken his way, making sure the bird doesn't suffer, and saying a little prayer, then it would be a sin for sure."

"Why," I asked.

"A long time ago in the old country the women would go to the village to pick their chickens for the Sabbath meal and the butcher would kill the chicken, in his way, always saying a prayer softly. The chicken never suffered and of course the butcher would charge for his services.

"One day, one of the women didn't feel well enough to walk to the village, so she asked her husband to go for her and pick out the plumpest chicken. 'Be sure that the butcher kills the chicken his way and pay him a little extra for his services,' the woman told her husband.

"The husband walked to the shop and picked out a fat chicken and then thought, 'I can save some money by killing the chicken myself. No one will know and my stupid wife will never guess!' So he paid for the live chicken, getting a puzzled look from the butcher, and took the chicken by its feet and proceeded home.

"He went straight to the barn, killed the chicken, plucked the feathers and presented the bird to his wife to cook. 'Did you pay the butcher for his services?' his wife asked. 'Yes, dear,' the man said, smiling and patting his pocket full of saved coins.

"After the Sabbath dinner, when all in his house were asleep, the man began to cough and cough. Each time he coughed feathers flew out of his mouth. He looked at his wife, sleeping soundly beside him. She did not wake. The coughing grew worse as the night passed.

"The next morning the wife awoke and found the bed covered with chicken feathers and no sign of her husband. Frightened, she ran to the village elders to tell them what she had found. The butcher, one of the elders, remembered that the husband had bragged to everyone what he had done, 'To save some coins,' the butcher told them sadly. 'And for this he was punished!'

"As this story passed from village to village the elders cautioned everyone. 'The traditions must be followed,' they said. And from that day to this no one has dared to break the traditions."

Every Friday from that day forward, I accompanied Bubbe Dear to the butcher. And when we paid for our chicken I asked the butcher, "Did you slay the chicken, say your prayer and are you sure she didn't suffer?" Then he would smile, touch his gray beard and nod his head.

And every Friday from that day forward, when we sat down to eat the Sabbath dinner, I discovered tiny yellow chicken eggs in my soup.

Once Bubbe Dear told about coming to America and her awful seasickness. "I spent most of the voyage hanging over the deck railing," she said. "Do you know, my precious, that every fish I saw in the ocean was an animal familiar to me?"

"You mean like a lion or a bear?" I whispered in amazement.

"Yes. Every day on that long voyage an animal appeared to me. The first was a lionfish with a big mane of yellow fur and a long tail. Then the tiger fish appeared. Oh, such beautiful stripes! Once I even saw an elephant fish. I could hardly believe my eyes! I was so fascinated by the animal fish I forgot to be sick!" Then Bubbe Dear smiled at me.

"But Bubbe Dear, I have never seen such fish in the ocean."

"Well," she asked, "did you travel across the ocean to America in a ship from the old country?"

"No, but I've been swimming in the ocean many times and never seen such exciting animals!" I must admit that I had begun to eye Bubbe Dear with mounting suspicion.

Ah," she spoke with the look of great pity on her face, "you have to come from the old country to see such unusual fish."

"Did you see a monkey fish or a giraffe fish?" I asked after a moment.

She wiped her hands on her apron and looked at me nodding. "Sure I saw them," she said. "The monkey fish even chatted with me. So cute, just like you, my pretty one. And would you believe, the giraffe fish had such a long neck he could see into the porthole of my cabin on the ship."

Well, that convinced me. Bubbe Dear always knew best. Once again I was a true believer.

As I grew older, weird things just seemed to happen when I was around. My mother would ask, "Who spilled the milk?" or "Who wrote on the living room wall?" or "Who took Uncle Moishe's teeth and hid them?"

"I don't know," I would answer her. "I didn't do it!"

Exasperated, mother would look at me and say, "I guess we must blame your invisible friend?"

One day, after my imaginary friend had been especially naughty, Bubbe Dear sat me down beside her.

"Along time ago in the old country," she said, "there lived little spirits who caused all kinds of mischief. If a person believed in them, their little tricks would cause no real harm. But if a person didn't believe, they would cause bad mischief. They were known to fly around the countryside doing their mischief and I think they have even caused wars.

"Well, there came a time when some of the people in the old country wanted to leave and go to America, to make a new life for themselves. When they left the little spirits traveled with them. Finally, after a long time at sea, the immigrants and their invisible spirits, arrived at Ellis Island.

"The spirits were restless after being confined on the ship and could hardly wait to start mischief making and cause confusion. Oh, they had a great time! Names were misspelled and some even changed completely. Bundles of belongings vanished while the immigrants waited on Ellis Island and after they moved into cold water flats on the east side of New York City. So many people and no one could understand anyone else's language. The mischievous spirits had a field day!"

When she had finished her story, Bubbe Dear got up to do some chores, but she left me wondering, each time I was tempted to do some mischief, if one of these spirits could be me? After that, when mother was cross or dad had a bad day at work, Bubbe Dear and I would look at each other knowingly – their spirits had caused it for sure.

Bubbe Dear once told me that her brother was slow witted and not quite right in his mind. I didn't understand what she meant, but I knew Uncle Moishe sat by the window everyday, laughing to himself and eating chocolate bars. One day he noticed that I was in the room and he took his little black coin purse from his vest pocket, and gave me a nickel. "Buy a chocolate bar for yourself, child," he told me. I ran downstairs to the candy store on the ground floor of our building and bought a chocolate bar to share with my uncle. He laughed and his teeth wobbled up and down and I laughed with him. I decided that Uncle Moishe's spirit was a good spirit.

Bubbe Dear had a good spirit too, one who granted wishes. "Little one," she called to me one morning. "Last night I had a dream and in my dream my spirit whispered these numbers." She showed me a piece of paper on which she had written several numbers, then folded it up. She then tied the paper in a handkerchief with a fifty cent piece and handed it to me. "Give this to the pickle man," she told me. And I took the little bundle to the pickle man.

One day the pickle man gave me a little bundle in return. When I handed it to Bubbe Dear she smiled jubilantly and showed me the money in the bundle. "The spirits have granted my wish," she told me. Every time her spirit granted her wish in this way Bubbe Dear would buy me a treat – a book or a luscious charlotte russe to eat. Imagine my surprise years later when I realized that I had been running numbers for my Bubbe Dear!

In those days my underwear always had tiny red ribbons on them. If I had thought anything about it I guess I would have supposed that the ribbons were on when purchased. Then, one day, I saw my mother sewing a red ribbon on a new pare and I asked her why.

"Go ask your Bubbe Dear," mother told me, laughing, so I did.

"Bubbe Dear," I asked when I found her sitting on the stoop in front of our building, "why do I wear a small red ribbon on my underwear?"

"To ward off the evil eye," Bubbe Dear said. "A long time ago in the old country a small band of wanderers came to live among the villages. They lived in wagons like the Gypsies use to do, and although they looked like everyone else, there was one difference. They didn't like to see color, it seems it hurt their eyes.

"The Wanderers preferred everything to be black or white. They also disliked babies, small children, or any one that had good fortune. In fact, it seemed that they were jealous and envious of all around them. When they looked at someone they would cast an evil eye on that person – very bad luck indeed!

"The elders of one of the villages realized that the Wanderers could not stand to see color. So they went to the weavers of cloth and asked, 'What is your brightest color?' The weavers replied, 'Red'. 'Then weave us cloth of pure red,' the elders told the weavers, and they did.

"Next the elders took the red cloth to the tailors. 'Make this cloth into strips,' the elders said, and the tailors did as asked. Finally the elders took the strips of red cloth to the merchants and said, 'Sell this cloth to the people in small pieces so that they may pin the bits of red to their clothing.' And the merchants did as requested.

"Everyone in the village pinned a bit of red cloth to their clothing and to the clothing of their children. When the Wanderers saw this they fled the village, unable to produce their evil eye any longer.

"From that day on the people of the villages wore small strips of red to adorn their clothing. It is a tradition passed down through the years."

"And we must keep traditions," I said, nodding in understanding.

As a child I loved celebrating Chanukah. For eight days Bubbe Dear would give me a candle to light each night and I would find presents under the menorah – chocolate coins and toys.

One year, during the holiday season, mother took me to a department store where she shopped and I saw children sitting on Santa Claus' lap, whispering in his hear. I wanted to give him my secret list of wishes, too.

"Why can't I speak to Santa Claus, Mother," I asked and she said, "Ask Bubbe Dear." So I did.

"Granddaughter," she began, "Santa Claus is a busy elf at holiday time. A long time ago he took the list of children from around the world and tore it in half. He kept one half and gave the other half of the list to his cousin Harry. 'I'll visit the children on my half of the list at Christmas,' Santa told his cousin. 'You visit the other half of the list at Chanukah.'"

"Does Harry wear a red suit, too? What does he look like?"

"If Harry wore a red suit no one would be able to tell him from his cousin. No, he chose to wear blue, and although he also has a long white beard, Harry has two curled locks, one at each temple. Yes, Harry's the one brings you gifts at Chanukah."

Chanukah Harry. I liked that. "Where did Chanukah Harry come from, Bubbe Dear?"

"From the old country, a long time ago, precious. Where else?"

The following spring as Passover neared I didn't bother to ask mother about the Easter Bunny some of my friends talked about. I went straight to Bubbe Dear. I knew she would have an answer!

"In the spring, the Easter bunny shared his list of children with one of his many, many relatives," Bubbe Dear began her tale. "One in particular was called Passover Pam. She brought chocolate matzos to the children on her list, and other sweet treats. She also brought a new outfit to wear for the first Seder night and black patent leather sandals to go with it. Sometimes, if the weather in spring was too cool, she also brought a new spring coat and hat."

That sounded logical to me. On the first night of Passover, during the Seder, we sat at the dinner table and my father asked me to open the door for the Angel Elijah to enter. I walked to the door and opened it slowly, afraid of what I might see. But no one was in sight. I looked up and down the hallway in case he was hiding, but the angel didn't appear.

I had just returned to my chair when Bubbe Dear announced, "He has entered," and father poured a glass of wine for the guest to drink. I kept glancing at the glass to see if the wine level was going down, just in case I had missed his entrance, but nothing happened. Maybe Elijah was like Passover Pam, I thought, admiring my new dress and beautiful black patent leather shoes – invisible!

The evening was long and, I thought, long-winded. I didn't understand the significance of the feast at that age. After a few sips of wine, and with my stomach full, I fell asleep at the table, and father carried me to Bubbe Dear's bed.

"A long time ago in the old country . . ." – that's how I now begin each story for my own grandchildren. I have never thought my stories as colorful or good as Bubbe Dear's had been for me. However I must have absorbed something of her as I listened and learned about my heritage from her wit and wisdom. I believe I can see in my own grandchildren what she must have seen in me – the future.

Biography of
Michael Murphy

Michael J. Murphy, a graduate of North Eastern University in Boston, was an editorial assistant at the Boston Globe Newspaper, a television producer for many years at WBZ-TV, also in Boston, the NBC affiliate.

Later he owned and operated an advertising agency and film production company. A former Army officer, he served as an intelligence staff officer in the Washington D. C. area and later as a NATO international staff officer working outside Paris.

Michael was born and raised in Gardiner, Maine.

SONNET

Poem

by Mike Murphy

Now gone across the fields of silent thought
Where memories are petrified in place
A flowing figure in a gown of lace
Is moving with the glory I have sought.
And from that mystic vision to the last,
There yet remains a fresh familiar grace
Of warm eyes shining in a quiet face
And love that lived on after life had passed.

The ebb and flow of time may carry me
Down rows of days that run into a day
When I must tear this mask of life away
To find another love that is resigned
By natural laws to give a soul its peace,
Eternal from the moment of release

Biography of
Claudia Cunningham

Claudia Cunningham is the senior member of the Creative Writer's Group. A bit past ninety, Claudia's poems and stories are a delight to those fortunate enough to hear, or read them. She was born and raised in Pittsburgh, Pennsylvania. Claudia's father was a newspaperman, her mother a professional photographer. She says she's been seriously writing for only the past twenty years, all the other stuff she wrote before that time got dumped in the trash. Now the writer's group waits anxiously to hear her next poem, or short story that are always polished and elegant, full of wisdom and wicked wit.

LIFE IN A SARDINE CAN

Memoir

by Claudia Cunningham

It's spring and we have moved into a lovely warm fourth floor walk-up three bedroom apartment that's small enough for our second-hand furniture to be in scale. The little place is a breeze to clean.

There are lots of people around: three hundred plus we two in the five buildings of the complex. We hear them fighting, yelling out of the windows to their kids below who are yelling back up, babies crying, phones; ringing, etc. I have never lived like this before and I find it amazing!

We hear stuff we really don't want to hear like the heavy lady below us who uses a snowdrift of white powder dusted all over her face, lips a scarlet gash, and the voice of a stevedore that easily penetrates our floor boards as she shouts, coos and flirts with various gentlemen on the phone after her husband leaves in the morning.

We never see these afternoon lovers as she always goes out at two o'clock and returns at five to bang around her kitchen with her cooking utensils. When her poor exhausted husband arrives at six p.m. covered with plaster dust and coughing, she screams at him, "You no-good! Why are you just standing outside the door? Take off our shoes in the hall . . . I don't want plaster all over my floor. I've been scrubbing a day! You good-for-nothing! Why do I put up with you?"

And on, and on it goes while she serves him dinner. We really never hear his voice, only a deep racking cough. The arguments are all one-sided.

One day I peeked over the hall banister because I'm so curious it's killing me, and I see a thin little man with bowed shoulders, dressed in grey cover-alls and cap, slowly and painfully descending the stairs, one at a time, while she yells at him all the way to the bottom.

That afternoon about four thirty, there's a terrible screaming and wailing out on the stairs and everyone in all the apartments rush out onto their landing to see what is the matter. Our downstairs neighbor is leaning over her banister, pulling her hair and sobbing and screaming, "Yakob! Yakob! Come back! Oh! My God, why are you taking him from me?"

"What's going on?" everyone is asking, looking up the stairwell.

"My Yakob! The best husband a woman could have! Such a wonderful man! They phoned me that he is dead! Killed in an explosion! Oye vey!"

She starts screaming again, pulling out tufts of her blonde-dyed hair and sobbing wildly.

Now the stairs are crowded with tenants from other buildings. "No!" "What is it?" "Terrible."

I go back inside our apartment and call the woman manager, a retired nurse, and tell her that the woman is hysterical and she comes, leads the woman inside her apartment, and gives her a shot to calm her down. Everyone else departs, murmuring to each other in horrified tones. Finally, silence is restored.

At six p.m. there is the sound of footsteps dragging up the stairs and the sound of the door below opening.

"Oh! My God! You are a ghost!" Screams follow.

"Woman! What do you say? I am your husband, Yakob!"

"No! No! Yakob's dead! He was killed this afternoon! Don't touch me! Don't touch me! It's forbidden!"

"Who told you such a thing?" he demands.

"They called me and said you were killed in an explosion!"

"What explosion?"

"Where you were working ... a gas explosion! They asked for Mrs. Feldstein and when I said 'Yes', they said you were killed in an explosion where you worked."

There are a few seconds of stunned silence.

"There must be another Yakob Feldstein. God have mercy, poor man! I'm fine and hungry. Where is supper?"

"You good-for-nothing! You hoodlum! Worrying me like that. You no-good!" and a steady stream of abuse as the door closes and I hear a bout of painful coughing from the husband a great clattering of pots and pans.

Life downstairs is back to normal.

CHERI

I had not lived in the mobile park long when I heard about Cheri for the first time. That June afternoon was lovely and I lazily napped, lying on my back on the swing with my feet propped up on the armrest, my mouth open and drooling – not my most charming position!

Suddenly someone knocked on the screen door. "Sorry to alarm you," a deep voice said. "I just wanted to get acquainted."

I got up hurriedly and as I opened the door he handed me a carton of cold beer.

"I'm Richard from up the street – the house with the crooked palm tree in front."

I quickly swept all the magazines off the plastic wicker table as Richard stretched out in one of the flowered plastic upholstered aluminum rockers – everything here is washable, non-rusting and non-mildew-able!

I had barely uttered a greeting when he continued. "Have you met your next-door neighbor yet? Eric is a gentleman of the highest moral fiber – so proper it hurts. A nice guy, divorced, and therefore tight with a buck – used to throw it away!"

Richard turned his head toward the next mobile and yelled, "Hey, Eric! Wake up! We need you!"

We could hear rustling from inside Eric's mobile, then he appeared carrying a tray filled with tiny veggie-spread crackers and rolled-up sandwiches. He was a supple six-footer with suntanned legs, glowing with muscles, and blond hair gleaming. When he came onto my porch he deposited the tray on the table and took a beer.

"He thinks he's making gourmet food when he spreads gook on a chip," Richard said with a teasing grin. "Just have to put up with it if you want to keep him happy!"

Eric sat in the other rocker, pointed to the roast beef roll-ups and looked at me. "Those'll put hair on your chest," he said with a straight face.

Richard popped one of the roll-ups into his mouth and was about to take two more when he exploded into a coughing fit.

"What the hell is in these?" he yelped.

"Wassabe – you know – Japanese horseradish," Eric explained with an innocent aggrieved tone, his wicked grin spoiling the effect! "Last time you said you liked horse-radish with your roast beef!"

Richard wheezed and looked at me. "What's your name honey?"

"Oh! Honey will do, although I usually go by Claudia," I said.

Richard had stopped coughing by now, after a couple of gulps of beer. ""Don't think I ever heard that name before." I started to respond, but he turned to Eric. "Why don't we all go swimming at Eaton's Beach later?"

"Went this morning," Eric stated. "Fish bit me!"

"Old Whoosis usually feeds the gators and big fish early in the morning before the bathers get there," Richard told me. "Otherwise the fish nibble at your legs so you have to keep moving."

"Sounds scary," I replied.

"No, you get used to the red marks," he said, chuckling. "Its just unexpected. You can always tell the new folks by the sudden yelps!"

"What about the gators?" I asked, worried.

"I was just kidding – nobody is allowed to feed them because they won't be afraid of people if you do. Anyway, they all hang out down at the swampy end of the lake – pretty exclusive bunch."

Eric rolled his eyes and I laughed and took another veggie do – dad. "Did you make these ahead of time?" I asked him.

"Yes, this is all pre-arranged. We just wanted to get to know you."

"It's a lovely way to do it – a party and I don't have to do a thing but provide chairs!"

Eric turned to Richard. "Heard you and Doc are on the outs over the local beauty!"

Richard laughed. "There was knock on the door and I yelled 'Come I' and she did. She was red in the face from sunburn and her arms and legs were scorched. She asked to use the bathroom, then came out naked! I told her to go back and put on her playsuit. She pouted and tried to get chummy and I went in and got her stuff and tossed it at her and told her to dress herself. She didn't take kindly to this treatment. She walked out of the house naked, went next door to Doc's and banged on his door, but there was no answer. So she tossed her clothes up in the air, letting them fall where they may, stuck her tongue out at me and trotted home 'au natural'! Next thing, Doc came out of his mobile and raised hell with me about throwing her clothes in his yard and I told him where to put them. So we aren't drinking buddies any more. Women always mess things up in my life.

I ignored this last and asked, "You mean she walked home naked? Who is she?"

"You haven't met Brother Ned and Sister Cheri, our local Bacchants?"

"Oh!" I replied, realization dawning, "You mean the pair in the new mobile down two streets? I met her walking barefooted over all those sharp stones on the road and singing to herself."

"Yep, that's her," Richard said.

"She looked a bit grungy."

"Never takes a bath alone," he added, shaking his head.

"She must have run out of partners – her dress was badly soiled and her hair was wild."

She can look ravishing when she's in the mood, but not lately," Richard said. "Their parents were killed in an automobile accident and the two inherited a large fortune. However, they were wild as kids and the will named watch-dogs to keep them from spending everything all at once. Cheri is on the 'sauce' and Brother Ned is 'riding the tiger'!"

"What does that mean?"

"She's an alcoholic and he's on drugs – goes around silent and practically paralyzed most of the time. They spend their whole allowance in a week and have a ball until it runs out. Then she latches onto some poor soul and makes his life a hell until the next check comes in and she's off to greener pastures far away. This mobile home in the park is their guardian's latest attempt at straightening them out, but Cheri managed to get arrested the second day after they moved in. Shoplifting – just waltzed out a liquor store with a fifth under each arm after grabbing the clerk and planting a big kiss on the dazed guy. She can be pretty charming and persuasive when she want to be."

Now I was really curious. "How old is she?"

"Nineteen. She and Ned are twins. Old enough to know better and young enough not to care!"

I met Louise later that week. She invited me for tea and I discovered, as we sat on her porch eating cinnamon toast, that the twins lived right next door.

We were interrupted by a loud banging around in the twin's mobile, and then screams. Just as we went outside to investigate Cheri came running across to us, crying and holding her hands out, palms up. We could smell smoke.

"Please help me," she cried. Both hands and arms were scarlet and puffing up in gray bubbles of skin.

"What happened," I asked as Louise ran to Cheri's mobile to check out the smoke. I didn't know what to do. Clearly the girl needed medical attention.

"I was taking the steak out of the broiler and it tilted and poured hot grease all over me. I dropped the pan on the floor but it caught fie and I couldn't get the fire out. I tried, but then I caught on fire, too!"

Louise returned then. "The fire is out. I turned off the stove. It's a mess in there."

"We need to get to a hospital right away," I told my new friend.

"I'll take her to the hospital in Ocala," Louise volunteered.

"I'll clean up the mess," I said, but Louise shook her head.

"We can clean it up later. I think I may need your help."

So the two of us took Cheri to the hospital in Ocala where they began her treatment.

I was at Louise's again about a week later, enjoying the cool evening under an oak tree, when Cheri walked over. She had soiled bandages on her feet and her arms were still wrapped, too. In my opinion she should have been in the hospital.

"You two are just the nicest people," she said to us, gushing. "Thanks so much for helping me. They let me go – I can't stand hospitals. I had to promise to go back in next week to have the bandages off." She waved her bandaged hands around overhead in a victory salute of some sort.

"How do you feel?" I asked.

"Oh! They keep me happy with pills. Not allowed alcohol, but the pills are great!"

The next time I saw her, the bandages were off and the new skin on her arms and feet was thin and pink and so fragile looking. Even then she walked around barefoot.

"I can't stand shoes," she told me merrily when she saw me looking at her feet.

"Your feet will become infected," I warned her. "They are already dirty. Why don't you stay in doors until they are healed?"

"Hate being trapped indoors," she replied sashaying a curtsy and walking off home.

A month later I awoke to hear a horrible rat-a-tatting sound all around my mobile.

"What on earth?" I couldn't imagine what was happening,. The clock said a quarter to six and that meant pre-dawn!

Then came a pounding on my door. I looked cautiously out the window and saw Cheri standing there.

"Sleepy head! It's a new day," she shouted when she saw me. "Let's celebrate – come out and dance in the dew-wet grass!"

More than a little annoyed I blinked and croaked out a hello as I opened the door to her. "What's this all about?"

"Oh! You were so sweet to me that I bought you a house warming present! Want to see it?" She popped in the door and handed me a huge flat package.

I tore away the wrapping and found a four-foot long painting of an Alpine lake, complete with mountains – one of those 'starving artist' types. Overwhelmed, I didn't know what to say, but the surprised expression on my face must have been enough to please her. She gave a huge hug and said "Enjoy!" and left.

"Cheri," I murmured, "you are full of surprises.

Sometime later I saw Cheri, blowing on a grass blade between her fingers, trying to make it whistle, she said. A little yellow butterfly kept circling her head.

"You seem so happy today," I told her. "Like a child!" And indeed that's what she reminded me of.

"Now is all we have," she said then. "Let's enjoy it."

I don't think I ever remember her being so pensive as that day.

"Violence and meanness belong to the outside world," she continued. "We make our own inside world and I want it to be happy and loving and serene."

"And when it isn't?" I asked.

"Then I go to Ned and we put our arms about each other and I weep and he kisses away the tears and licks my cheek and it tickles me and I have to laugh. He understands and is so gentle as he comforts me. And if it is really bad for me, he croons our song – the one we made up long ago as children when nobody cared for us. When were punished we would sing it together and make up verses."

She hummed a little tune then stopped. "He's lost, you know, Ned is lost. He says he is lost and can never find his way back and he lives in the gray would wandering about hopelessly – the drugs dull the lonely ache, I think. And then I comfort him and sing to him and we fall asleep and leave the world behind."

My heart ached to hear her melancholy tale. How lonely they must feel, how cut off from anyone, everyone.

"We are two halves of a whole and comfort each other and heal. We are twins, you know. I guess it all began in the womb, rocking in the warm darkness, hearing our mother' heart beating, the singing liquids in her arteries, the gurgles of intestines, and the squeaks of muscles."

"You never fight?" I asked after a long pause when she said nothing more.

"Oh! We yell at each other and tumble around and kick, but it passes and it never means much. Mostly it's because I haven't done the dishes or laundry and he is such a fuss-fidget about cleanliness. I'm such a slob he can't believe it! Or I make a wonderful steak dinner and he can't eat – really, physically can't eat – and I get so angry because all the effort is in vain, then I yell at him. But mostly it's just noise."

"Enjoy God's world while you can," she said finally. "All goes so fast – joy, sunshine, bliss, whatever you call it."

Cheri leaned over and put her palm against my cheek, then turned and walked on down the road.

Sometime after that I went north to visit friends and when I got back Louise told me that Ned had blown his brains out while Cheri was shopping for a special supper for his birthday. Cheri had left. I never saw her again.

Biography of
Lois Mayo

It's hard to believe that anybody as pretty as Lois Mayo could be a hard-working, serious writer. That's how it is, even though Lois has just taken up writing and has attended several writing courses and seminars. Yet, even without all the technical 'stuff', she is a very good story teller and the creative group is always amused at the humor when she reads her latest work, or scene's from her mystery novel. Born in New Jersey, she and Travis, her husband of twenty-five years have lived in Florida for many years.

THE BIRTHDAY CAKE

Memoir

by Lois Mayo

When Jane's first grandson turned two she had offered to bake the birthday cake. It was a small party so Jane baked a sheet cake and decorated it with a drawing on top of the little guy pushing a vacuum cleaner – pushing a vacuum was Johnny's favorite thing to do. Actually, he drove his mother crazy with this noisy obsession. The cake was a big hit.

Thus began the ritual. Grandma became more experienced as the number of grandkids grew – even taking a course in cake decorating and investing in all sorts of books and utensils to do the job right. It seemed that everyone came to each birthday party eager to see what she had created. To herself she admitted that, although she loved doing something special for each grandchild, she especially liked the attention she received with each cake!

When Grady's eighth birthday was planned his mother invited 25 kids and 14 parents, so Grandma knew she had to bake a large cake. With the party theme of "Nemo" from the Disney film, she decided to copy the adorable clown fish for the top of the cake and set out baking three days before the party.

The result was a masterpiece. The three layers of chocolate cake were covered in sea blue butter cream frosting. The base had green sea grasses and yellow coral fingers growing out of the confectionery bottom of the ocean. When all was ready she placed "Nemo" on the top – orange and white with a black strip – Perfect!

"By golly," she thought. "This is the best cake I've ever made. Wait until they see this one!"

The next day Jane and her husband carefully loaded the cake in the back seat of the car. Mindful of the cake, he drove very slowly around the corners so it wouldn't slide. Jane held Murphy, their little dog, on her lap all the way to their daughter's house.

When they arrived the children came running.

"Where's the cake, Grandma," Grady asked excitedly.

"Be patient, Grady," she admonished, grinning. "Let Grandpa get it out of the car!"

Grandpa opened the back door and reached in for the cake. Then suddenly, with the speed of lightning, Murphy jumped in right on top of the cake! Grandpa tried to grab the dog but Murphy was too quick. His little feet never touched the cake – which was covered with many layer of plastic wrap – but they smashed the cake nevertheless. To Jane's horror little Nemo was no more! The fancy sea grasses and coral rock fingers were smeared into oblivion!

For a moment everyone stood speechless, then suddenly began to laugh – even Grady, who at least tried to hide his laughter by covering his mouth. Jane looked at the cake then at her grandson and laughed, too.

"Well, if the birthday boy doesn't mind I won't worry either," she thought.

They carried the smashed creation to the kitchen and her daughter got out a couple of spatulas. Together they pushed the layers back together and smoothed the icing over the whole mess. Jane looked in dismay at the three – tiered glob covered with gray icing – the result of the mixing of the blue and orange.

"This is not working," she told her daughter. "I'm running to the supermarket to get a cake. I'll be right back."

"Don't you dare!" her daughter stated firmly. "This is the greatest conversation piece we've ever had!"

To Jane's amazement her daughter's prediction came true. With the arrival of each guest Grady took great delight in showing off his birthday cake and explaining what had happened to it.

Once again Grandma's cake was a huge hit! Especially the top which read – "Hap Birt Grady!"

Biography of
Thomas E. Leonard

Thomas Leonard came to the Villages from Jackson, Wisconsin. Tom was raised and grew up in the Midwest. He received an advanced degree from The University of Iowa. Scientific in nature, Tom, since retirement, enjoys writing stories that involve technical oddities and improbable dreams. He writes with expertise and great humor and is presently working on a memoir for his children and grandchildren.

JUST AN AVERAGE JOE

Fiction

by Thomas E. Leonard

Dr. Joseph Smith was the most average-above average person I've ever had the pleasure of knowing. He was average height, average weight and average build. He had the kind of average look that's impossible to describe and usually the first to forget. His crop of average brown hair was always going nowhere and even his name was average. Just count the number of Joe Smiths listed in the phone book. He had blue eyes, not especially handsome and a big ski-slope nose with the strangest looking big black-rimmed glasses, and a pointy chin. He was no head turner, but found himself a beautiful wife who was his best friend and helpmate and together they raised three wonderful kids. Not surprisingly he earned average grades in high school and college, but did manage to squeak out a doctors degree in chemistry at the University of Iowa.

Although Joe was average in most aspects of his life, he was above average at daydreaming. It's as though his mind was always somewhere else. Before talking to him, you had to first tune him in with either eye or hand contact – preferably both. If his eyes began to wander, you knew you were in trouble; the topic of conversation would abruptly switch to something he was 'reminded of", something which often had no connection to the present conversation, but was usually interesting. After graduation from university he became a teacher, and with a mind like his, how he managed to teach effectively I'll never know, but he did manage to get the 'teacher of the year' award three times.

We've known each other since grade school and went through college together, but while he chose teaching as a profession, I chose to get a real job as a lawyer complete with a comfortable salary. Joe was an inventor at heart and was always coming up with new ideas that usually seemed to involve me. I enjoyed helping Joe with some of his weird projects and he seemed to enjoy using me as his sounding board. He claimed he could tell what I thought of his ideas by the sparkle in my eyes. Actually I think those were tears in my eyes. Most of his ideas were really off the wall.

His biggest and most persistent dream was that of perfecting a perpetual motion machine – and he almost did! Perpetual motion machines seem to be the invention of choice for guys like Joe. His dream started in grade school and evolved to a degree of reality years after graduating from college. It was a long journey, but the evolution and development of his ideas made for some interesting side trips.

During our earlier years, when not playing baseball, we tinkered with small gasoline engines for our model airplanes. We went through high school together. Joe was president of the science club and I lettered in baseball. In high school science we learned that hydrogen is an explosive gas and can be separated from water by simply applying an electrical current to the liquid. That's when it happened. Joe got his all consuming, great idea; a perpetual motion machine. With a generator connected to the motor, he thought, the motor could generate electricity to produce the hydrogen necessary to run the motor, burning the hydrogen to form the water and back to hydrogen and on it goes. Wow, you wouldn't even need to re-supply the water in this devise. Electricity to water making hydrogen, which runs the motor producing electricity and so on: non-stop. A self-contained, self-running unit so he thought. He was so enthusiastic and convincing in his argument he managed to convince me of the idea. My eyes sparkled at the idea of free energy. That seemed to be the most normal, logical idea he's had since I knew him, I thought. It's amazing how one thing leads to another.

It didn't take long for his great idea to crumble. Laws governing the real world began to overtake those of the ideal world and, after a few tests, we both soon realized that not only can you not get something for nothing, when it changes forms, you can't even break even. That, I recalled, was a law I learned in economics classes about money and he learned in physics about energy. Heat, motion, even light and sound are all forms of energy and with these changes, energy is lost. It's like money, "you don't get something for nothing and, when it changes hands, you can't even break even". I certainly didn't break even after buying all those parts needed to try the dumb thing. I was ready to give up at that point, but not average-above-average Joe. Although he did drop the perpetual motion idea for the time being, he began to search of inexpensive forms of energy. I wasn't surprised when he got caught up with the environmental craze; sitting in trees, boycotting oil, marches, he even connected up with a commune for a while. About the time I thought he was lost forever he moved away from the eccentric life and into the more fruitful aspects of environmental issues: mostly energy related. He spent about ten years altogether with his environment thing and in his off time investigating the various energy machines touted by different investigators. Wind, tides, heat, solar energy, he tried them all.

In 1976, he received a grant from General Motors to construct a car that would run only on solar energy. Joe successfully constructed a very small, lightweight, single passenger car covered with solar panels that managed to run about one thousand miles in a bit less that twenty-eight hours. I helped him with some of the mechanics and he did the electronics. Except for the initial cost of the car and solar cells, the energy from the sun was "free". Although boring the good thing about that trip, he told me afterwards, was that he realized the abundant amount of solar energy available just begging to be harnessed and, although the cost of the "fuel" was free, a $120,000 dollar investment in solar panels to operate a slow moving, single passenger car wouldn't do it.

It took several hours and many drinks before he began to pontificate, "Cost, in general, is directly related to energy consumption," he said. "You don't get something for nothing, but solar energy is free. If only I could harness it at a low cost".

About two months after his trip he came to me with his revised dream. He was gushing with enthusiasm, which was nothing new for Joe. "Cover our city highways, sidewalks and roofs with one big affordable, energy efficient solar panel," he said. Think of all the solar exposure we could collect and energy produce! The sun provides about 4,000 kilowatts of energy on each mile of roadway which could provide about 250 homes with electricity. It's almost as if God has been laughing at us all these years. I can just hear him or her, with that big booming voice in the sky: 'I gave you all this energy and you've been wasting your time, getting your hands dirty; digging holes in the ground and playing with that oily muck'. Think of all the energy we're losing on those bare roadways; and we add about a million acres to urban development, highway and airports each year, 3.5 billion acres worldwide. If only it could be harnessed."

'*Arg!*' I thought abnormally-normal Joe was at it again. This time there were tears in my eyes.

It was about six months after his infamous "revised dream" episode when the Smiths had us over for a Thanksgiving dinner. No sooner did we arrive than Joe grabbed me by the arm and rushed me to a corner where he expounded on his latest discovery: an asphalt-like material that produces an electric current when exposed to light.

"Light is energy," he mused, "and wherever there's light there's energy available for the taking."

He then proceeded to explain in more detail than I needed, about this latest material he concocted. This material, when layered on top of a recently produced concrete that conducts electricity, would produce a current. He then showed me his plan to construct photocells that could be laid down just like asphalt at a cost of only about ten percent more than the normal road cover. The "show" was indeed very exciting. When he gets going, his enthusiasm is infectious and I was infected. He took me down to his basement laboratory replete with the average mess and brought out a can of black goo and a can of clear goo. First he poured the black mess onto a bed of sand and hurriedly plunged a wire into the stuff. After a few minutes of drying time, he poured the clear liquid over the black goo and stabbed a second wire into it. Another few minutes and the whole mess was as hard as a rock. He took the solid mass over to a bright light and hooked the protruding wires up to an ammeter and voila, it registered enough current to power a small motor. He then showed me, with a few simple calculations, that a few miles of this hardened goop on a sunny day could provide enough power for a small town.

"Beats using the sun to heat concrete," he said.

Wow! I was impressed.

He then proceeded to hit me with the financial end of his problem: he needed money, big time and that look on his face told me I was about to be his first big hit, or so he thought. All he had to do was find a financial backer. I don't think he expected me to back him completely, but I have often gone in and lost money on some of his other wild projects and this was too good to pass up, but at that time I was financially strapped. He figured all he needed was about half a million to "try" it. Gulp.

We were in the midst of funding our kids' college educations and no way could I even put a dent in that kind of budget requirement. "Have you looked for an outside investor," I asked, somewhat jokingly.

"Yes, I've thought about it, but frankly I'm afraid. I recall, too well, the story of how, GM, Firestone, and Standard Oil bought out the trolley business and then shut it down in order to get more cars on the road. There's so much greed out there and I just want to save the world."

I thought that sounded like a typical above average comment from my average Joe. What a guy! He was smiling when he said it though and that was good. Was he just kidding?

Fortunately our conversation was interrupted with a call from upstairs for dinner followed by our usual foray with pinochle. It gave us both time to think while our wives proceeded to win all five games – as usual. It was late by the time we completed our games and I was glad to leave without going on with Joe about his project and financing. It was a lot for me to handle and I needed time to sort it out.

As we left I simply signaled Joe and said, "I'll be in touch about the . . . ." my voice dribbled away. Frankly I was scared. Joe, I thought, out did himself this time and I wasn't sure if I wanted to be even a tiny part of this latest venture. I didn't think I could handle a project that big, but it did sound inviting.

It took a little longer than a week before we got together again for our big discussion about his latest project and how to make it happen. We met at O'Hannon's Irish Pub our favorite place, nice and quiet and served free pretzels with beer and the greatest pizza. The only things Irish about the place was the green beer Tony Boccocini, the owner, served on St. Patrick's Day and the funny green top hat he wore behind the bar, like he was Irish or something. I came prepared just in case, with my calculator, pen and lots of paper. I was calm at first, just sitting and waiting for Joe to show, but felt a rush of anxiety when Joe came stumbling in with his trusty worn-out briefcase, an armful of papers and a few books.

'*This is it,*' I thought. '*Can I turn back? Could I say no to my best buddy? I can't do this.*'

He bellied up to the bar, ordered a pitcher of beer and came over to the table with a big grin on his face. I was wishing, hoping if only . . . .

"Did you find some money," I asked.

"No, but I'm pumped."

Never mind that he spilled beer on his papers and I already had a pitcher on the table. '*We'll need two pitchers this night anyhow,*' I thought. Not surprisingly, before I could woof down a second glass, Joe began with his treatise and I soon became infected with his meticulously detailed data. Not only did he have a plan for his mile long test strip, but h also showed how he could plug into the national utility grid plus store excess electricity for cloudy days and the real kicker: a proposal for a hydrogen economy.

'*Wow,*' I thought, '*he's got it all together. I wonder what he does in his spare time.*'

His ever-present enthusiasm and sincere belief in his latest idea sold me. I gave up. I convinced myself. I guess it's a go. Together we pored over all his papers, the latest research, his notes, current technology and finally dollar figures.

'*Finally,*' I thought, '*something I know something about.*'

Amazingly, he did manage to trim his initial cost estimates to $200,000, but we both agreed, with concerns about patent protection and privacy, outside funding would be difficult. With an ultimate source of truly free energy what companies would profit, which ones would not and what would that do to the economy? As a patent lawyer I could foresee potential challenges with big business; maybe even the government and that cost money – big time.

No concrete answers, no firm plan of attack, but we polished off the two pitchers of beer and ended our two and a half hour communion with a lot of laughs and fun with a full range of what-if scenarios. The corny jokes, crazy stories coupled with the great pizza and beers and pretzels under our belt seem to give us the proper attitude for an all out was with this crazy, seemingly impossible adventure. Good thing we both lived within walking distance of O'Hannons.

Biography of
Nance Ann Holinko

Nance Ann Holinko's career as a author began after retirement. In the business world she was known for her wit, savvy and an occasional 'sharp pen'.

After moving to Florida, Nance's husband died as did DJ, her beloved pet, so Nance turned to writing. Her first book, *A BARK AND A BOOK*, chronicled her life with her husband, but with a slight twist: The dog writes the book! And it's available at local bookstores.

WHAT'S IN A NAME?

Memoir

By Nance Holinko

My parents, or more truthfully my Mother, a got a bit confused about names for her children. Embarrassingly there were only three, but she made a total and confusing mess of what should have been a simple matter.

I was the first born – a long wait had ensued prior to my arrival. Eight years, in fact, so there should have been no problem. Yet, ever since my mother had been a wee lassie, she had named all her dolls 'Nancy'. So when I came into the picture it was predestined that I would inherit that name. Unfortunately, this was early Catholic times and the church had ruled that all Catholic children should be named for a saint. Alas, there was no Saint Nancy and a discussion followed that perhaps eventually I would qualify for the esteemed title. Finally, my father intervened decreeing that I would be named after his mother Elizabeth and for good luck, my mother's name, Ann would be added.

Thus it happened at age sixteen when I went looking for my birth certificate, I discovered to my dismay that 'Nance' did not exist. I was Ann Elizabeth. No kidding. Adding to the confusion, I had fudged my birthday by a year.(When you're in your teens, you can't wait to be twenty! Right?) Then to really stir up the pot, I had made a bet with a friend, a Notre Dame guy, no less, that I was old enough to enjoy a glass of whisky with him and made a bet on the side that if I spelled my name Nance for a year, I would win a bottle of expensive Scotch whiskey. This was all I needed, a challenge and a rebuke to my mother for a name I didn't want. The whiskey is long gone, but the memory lingers still.

My brother Pete, the middle child, and far and away my mother's favorite, had arrived during an easy birth. His good looks suggested 'big wins' for all baby contests. No one could deny his charm and beautiful blue eyes. It was a foregone conclusion that he would be named Peter after my uncle (my father's brother) who had mysteriously perished working as a radio operator aboard a ship in the Atlantic ocean off the coast of South America. So, Peter got the name of a dead man.

At this point, my mother allowed me to help name the next baby. I had picked Wendy should the child have been a girl. I did suggest Jerome, which happened to be Peter's middle name, but somehow that brainstorm got ignored.

Brother Jim – well the poor kid was a star from the very beginning. He showed up my brother and me something awful. He was intelligent and well coordinated – a pure sportsman to this very day.

His baptism papers will tell you that his name is James Anthony, but in time, he became William, or William James. You figure. We just never could. And my mother who had taken on mysterious illegal names for herself, registered poor Jim in seven different colleges under a variety of names. Now he's a physician and I know he's not a quack, but each of his diplomas on his office wall states a different name. Combining his doctor training papers with a degree in engineering, one can imagine why patients leave his clinic office with puzzled looks.

As a postscript concerning my strange clan, I have to confess that mother and father's legal names (clearly written right there on their birth certificates) are Barbara and Vincent. Go Figure!